'Synod adopts and approves the draft BCO version 4 text, as submitted for consideration by the British Presbytery (incorporating the European proto-Presbytery) and the Korean Presbytery (incorporating the South Korean proto-Presbytery) and as amended by this Synod as the Book of Church Order of the International Presbyterian Church.'

Excerpt from Minute of Synod, London, 5th June 2015

Amended by order of Synod 10th June 2016

Amended by order of Synod 3rd March 2017

FIFTH EDITION
Issued 4th March 2017

BOOK OF CHURCH

ORDER

OF THE

INTERNATIONAL
PRESBYTERIAN CHURCH

CONTENTS

SECTION 1

THE OVERRIDING OBJECTIVE

1.1 The Overriding Objective: Pleasing the Lord Jesus Christ

The Overriding Objective of the Church is to please and glorify the triune God through his Son, our Lord and Saviour, Jesus Christ, who is the incarnate second person of the Trinity, crucified, risen, exalted, and reigning as Head of the Church, King of kings, and Lord of lords, by the power of the Holy Spirit. Therefore the Overriding Objective of the Book of Church Order is to equip the International Presbyterian Church to do this in its life and government.

Conducting Church government in a manner that pleases the Lord Jesus Christ includes:

(i)   being obedient to the teaching of God's Word, the Holy Scriptures of the Old and New Testaments;

(ii)   being submissive to that understanding of Scripture expressed by the Westminster Confession and Catechisms and the Three Forms of Unity, which are therefore known as our subordinate standards;

(iii)   making a priority of the faithful preaching the gospel of grace to the Church and to the world, the right administration of the sacraments, appropriate Church discipline, joyful worship, rich fellowship among believers, loving and sacrificial acts of service, and a witness of mercy and justice;

(iv)   making prayer a central component of any decision-making process and trusting the Holy Spirit to work in and direct the Church as she seeks to preach the gospel of grace and implement biblical law and wisdom;

(v)   pursuing a holy unity in the gospel in all decision making;

(vi)   being thankful in everything to God the Father, God the Son, and God the Holy Spirit.

1.2 Seeking to Give Effect to the Overriding Objective

The Synod, Presbyteries, Sessions, Diaconates and any Trustees must seek to give effect to the Overriding Objective when they exercise any of their powers or otherwise carry out any of their business.

1.3 Duty of the Members of IPC Congregations

The Members of IPC congregations are required to help their Session to further the Overriding Objective of pleasing the Lord Jesus Christ.

1.4 Power to Amend the Book of Church Order

The Book of Church Order (hereafter, BCO) may be amended only by Synod and in accordance with the Overriding Objective. Any amendments concerning church membership shall require consultation with the members of IPC churches.

SECTION 2

THE STRUCTURE OF THE CHURCH

2.1 Principles

Given that the Church is one, holy, catholic and apostolic, united as the single covenant people of God, it is appropriate for the Church to express her unity in the government of the Church.

The Scripture reveals this happening in councils of Elders, entrusted by Christ with the power to ordain and discipline Church Elders and to decide on matters of Church life and doctrine. The fact that such councils may err does not remove their necessity for the health and wellbeing of the Church.

Furthermore, Scripture shows that councils of Elders operate on three levels:
- Elders within each local church (Acts 20:17–38)
- Regional (1 Tim 4:14)
- Worldwide (Acts 15)

While a universal organisational unity of Christ's Church has not been possible for many centuries, we are nevertheless required by Christ to implement this structure as best we can, for it expresses in practice our unity and mutual accountability in Christ. At the same time, we recognise and rejoice in the fact that Christ's Church is vastly wider than

vote of those present and voting for or against a motion in a quorate meeting.

All special business shall be decided by a three-quarters majority of those present and voting for or against a motion in a quorate meeting[1].

Special business must be notified with the agenda in advance of a meeting and is defined as one of the following:

(i)   The appointment, transfer, removal and discipline of church officers in all councils of the church;

(ii)   Amendment of the BCO;

(iii) Remuneration of church officers;

(iv) Sale or purchase of land or major capital assets;

(v)   Other matters specifically identified as special business in a particular council of the church.

Voting in respect of ordinary business shall normally be by a show of hands. The moderator may, at his discretion accept a request for a secret ballot.

Special business shall normally be voted on by secret ballot.

2.2.1 Formal Decisions in Any Council

Formal decision making of the councils of the Church shall involve the submission of a competent **motion** to the clerk

---

[1] [For the Korean Presbytery the requirement shall be a two thirds majority of those present and voting]

of the council. A motion shall have a proposer and a seconder to be considered competent. In the case of a motion proposed from another Court, Commission or Committee of the Church, there shall be no requirement for a seconder. The proposer shall usually be the **mover** of a motion and is expected to give a short explanation of its purpose. A motion that contravenes any provision(s) of the BCO cannot be considered competent without reverting to the Synod. The rule of the moderator is final in this regard.

An **amendment** may be laid before the meeting during discussion/debate on a motion. An amendment should not fundamentally change the substance of the motion (when it should be considered a countermotion). An amendment shall require a proposer and a seconder. If acceptable to the mover, there need be no separate consideration — the amended motion becomes the substantive motion of discussion/debate. Where the mover does not agree to the amendment, the amendment shall be considered first and then voted on separately. If the amendment falls, the resulting original motion should then be debated.

After appropriate discussion/debate the motion shall be put to the council of the Church. The moderator shall rule on whether the vote is ordinary or special business.

The clerk shall record the results of the vote in the minutes.

Where a decision on a motion renders a subsequent motion irrelevant, the moderator may rule that the subsequent motion shall not be discussed.

The moderator shall have discretion to consider a **call to move to next business** which will terminate discussion on the current business without a vote and without the council coming to or expressing a view on it. The mover should be given opportunity to explain why the motion should be voted on. A call to move to next business requires a three-quarters majority of those present and voting.

SECTION 3

CHURCH MEMBERSHIP

Church membership in a local church is important in the life of a believer. Jesus said that he would build his Church and we see in Acts that the Apostles were baptising believers and bringing them into the Church. Indeed the Lord was adding to their number (Acts 2:41–42, 47). He is the Head of the Church, yet he has commissioned his people to go and make disciples. This process of making disciples is done through the work of the local church. Elders are called to shepherd those under their care (1 Pet 5:1–4, Acts 20:28) and the people of God are called to submit to them (Heb 13:17). Scripture also requires the people of God to bear one another's burdens and to do good especially to those who are of the household of faith (Gal 6:2, 10). In these ways, and in others, Scripture presumes a household of faith with some way for us to know who is in and who is out, and furthermore, who is in which congregation. Elders must know whom they are to shepherd; Christians must know to which Elders they are to submit; all of us must know which brothers and sisters we are particularly called to serve and love. God has designed Church membership for our good and growth in the gospel.

3.1 Communing Members of an IPC Congregation

In order to become a Communing Member (hereafter, referred to as 'a Member') of an IPC congregation, a person must:

(i)   have been baptised, whether as a child or an adult;

(ii)   demonstrate a credible profession of faith in the Lord Jesus Christ as their Saviour and Lord;

(iii)   have publicly declared and affirmed to the congregation their profession of faith and acceptance of membership, whether verbally or in writing;

(iv)   unless the Session otherwise allows, not be a Member of any other church.

The Session has the discretion whether or not to admit a person to membership as it sees fit in accordance with the above criteria.

Any candidate for membership who considers the Session has acted wrongly in the exercise of its discretion may appeal to the Presbytery.

3.2 Non-Communing Members of an IPC Congregation

Any child of one or both Communing Members of an IPC Congregation is, through the covenant and by right of birth, a Non-Communing Member of the same congregation to which his or her parent(s) belong(s) and therefore ought to be brought for baptism.

A Non-Communing Member is entitled to pastoral care, oversight, and instruction in the Lord.

Children growing up as Non-Communing Members should be taught the meaning of the gospel of Christ by their parents. This is the parents' responsibility, and the church should resource and support parents in this demanding task.

When parents believe that their child has a sufficient understanding of the gospel, they may ask the Elders to consider admitting the child to the Lord's Table.

A sufficient understanding of the gospel means an ability to examine him or herself as all Christians must do before coming to the Lord's Table. This includes understanding and believing:

(i)   that there is one God who is eternally three persons, Father, Son and Holy Spirit;

(ii)   that they are made in the image of God, yet like all mankind have fallen into sin;

(iii)   that Christ died on the cross to take the penalty for their sins, and was raised from the dead to give us eternal life;

(iv)   that God forgives the sins of those who trust Christ;

(v)   that real trust in Christ is always accompanied by repentance and a desire to live for him;

(vi)   that the Lord's Supper is a sign of how Christ gives us life by his death and resurrection, which we must believe if it is to be of value to us.

Having received a request from the parents, one of the Elders will meet with the child to ask him or her about his or her understanding of the gospel and the Lord's Supper. The Session will then discuss the child and either agree to admit the child to the Lord's Table or give the parents directions on further teaching and training that they need to give the child or maturity the child needs to develop before he or she can be admitted.

Appropriate discretion and judgment is to be used on the part of the Elders in this decision, having due regard to the child's character and ability, and aiming always at discerning genuine faith, as much as is humanly possible, rather than mere ability to give correct answers.

3.3 The Effect of Membership

Only persons who are Communing Members of the congregation and who have reached the age of 18 may vote in relation to that congregation's business or may raise an appeal to the Presbytery on any issue, doctrinal or otherwise, affecting the congregation of which the person is a Member.

Church Members need to consider carefully and review regularly their stewardship of all the resources God gives them. Time, money and skills are all gifts from God that we should joyfully and sacrificially share with the church.

Unless the Session permits in exceptional circumstances,

only Communing Members of the congregation may teach or mentor children or adults in that congregation.

Unless the Presbytery has permitted otherwise for a particular person, only persons who are Communing Members of the congregation are eligible to be called to the office of Elder or Deacon in that congregation.

Unless the chairman of a Congregational Meeting has permitted otherwise for a particular person, only Members of the congregation (whether communing or non-communing) may speak in public and call for proposals at such meetings.

Attention is drawn to the duty of Members to help the Session further the Overriding Objective (see section 1.3).

3.4 Membership Transfer and Termination

A Member of one IPC congregation may for good reason transfer their membership to another IPC congregation, in which case the Session of his or her new congregation shall admit that person's name to the Membership Record provided that there is no objection by the Session of his or her old congregation.

When an individual seeks transfer to an IPC church from another denomination, the reasons for the transfer should be made clear. Session may contact the previous congregation for information and to ensure no legitimate objection exists. The requirements for membership shall be as described in section 3.1.

Membership of an IPC congregation shall cease only in the following circumstances:

(i)   upon a Member's death;

(ii) upon a Member's transfer of membership to another congregation or church (in cases where the member's new church does not have a formal membership system, this shall be considered a transfer of commitment, and IPC membership shall not cease until the Session is satisfied after contact with the Member that cessation would be appropriate);

(iii)in a situation where the Session considers a Member to have left the congregation;

(iv)   upon the termination of membership by the Session.

3.5 Membership and Discipline Situations

(see also section 11)

Attention is drawn to it being part of the function of the Session to protect the purity of the Church and the honour of the Lord Jesus Christ in ways which are primarily ministerial not magisterial (in other words, appealing to the heart of an offending Member without resort to legal force); but this does not mean that the Session will refrain from reporting suspected criminal activity to the police or, in the case of a child at risk of harm from the suspected behaviour of a Member, to the appropriate state authorities; on the contrary, the Session will do so without delay in appropriate cases.

In the course of their pastoral care and oversight of

Members of the congregation, the Session may, from time to time, have to exercise careful and loving discipline.

The ultimate object of such discipline is the restoration and reconciliation of a Member who is being persistently and seriously disobedient to the Lord Jesus Christ.

Should a restoration become impossible, the Session may end the membership of such a person by excommunicating them, usually following the pattern of Matthew 18 in balance with all other Scripture.

3.6 Appeal to Broader Church Councils

One or more Members of a church who have concerns about one or more Elders' teaching, doctrine or life should raise them with the individual(s) concerned or, where necessary, discuss them with the Session. If resolution is not possible or such discussion is not appropriate they may appeal to Presbytery.

Where other problems of disagreement or conflict involving one or more Elders arise, Members should raise them with the individual(s) concerned or where necessary discuss them with the Session. If resolution is not possible or such discussion is not appropriate they may appeal to Presbytery.

Appeals to Presbytery should be made in writing to the Presbytery Clerk or Moderator. Presbytery has discretion over whether to admit an appeal for consideration or not.

Any Member or Elder (including the Session) involved, who considers the decision of the Presbytery to be erroneous having regard to the Overriding Objective, may appeal to Synod. Appeals to Synod should be made in writing to the Synod Clerk or Moderator. Synod has discretion over whether to admit an appeal for consideration or not.

3.7 Members' Meetings

3.7.1 The Nature of Members' Meetings

The main purpose of Congregational Meetings is for Members to have the opportunity to listen to and participate in honest discussion in a spirit of love, with a view to reaching substantial agreement about what may please the Lord on the issues to be decided.

Adequate notice and draft agenda of the meeting shall be given to the Members to allow time to bring comments and proposals to the Session.

The meeting shall be chaired by an Elder from the Session or by a person appointed by the Session. Where there is no Session, the meeting will be chaired by a person appointed by Presbytery.

Congregational Meetings shall usually be open to the public, but no persons other than church Members may speak without being invited to do so by the chairperson.

A note-taker will prepare a summary of the salient points ('minutes') which must be provided to all Members of the congregation; such minutes shall be treated as a true and fair record if no objection is made by anyone within one month of distribution. If there are objections, the matter shall be dealt with at the next meeting, and the draft minutes shall not be approved except by congregational vote at that meeting or otherwise.

Votes in Members' meetings shall only be cast in person by those Members present at the point when the vote is being taken, unless the Session allows otherwise in exceptional circumstances (for example, a house-bound Member).

A quorum of any Members meeting shall be one third of those eligible to vote.

All ordinary business shall be decided by a simple majority vote of those present in a quorate meeting.

All special business shall be decided by a three-quarters majority of those present in a quorate meeting.

Special business is one of the following:

(i) The appointment or approval of church officers;

(ii) Remuneration of church officers;

(iii) Sale or purchase of land or major capital assets;

(iv) Separation of the church from the denomination.

Voting in respect of ordinary business shall normally be by a show of hands. The moderator may, at his discretion, accept a request for a secret ballot. Special business shall normally be decided by secret ballot.

3.7.2 The Frequency of Members' Meetings

The Session will convene at least one Members' Meeting every year, which must be an Annual General Meeting. Additional 'Extraordinary Meetings' may be called as required.

At the Annual General Meeting the business of the meeting shall include:

(i)   the Session's review of the preceding year and outlook for the following year;

(ii)   a prayerful reflection on church activities of the preceding year;

(iii)   the presentation of the annual accounts and budget of the congregation by the treasurer;

(iv)   any other appropriate matters.

3.7.3 Procedures

At any Members' Meeting any Member or Elder may call for a proposal to be put to a vote, provided that:

(i)   the meeting has a quorum;

(ii)   the proposal directly concerns the subject matter under discussion;

(iii)   the Session approves.

If the Session does not approve of, or give conditional approval to, putting a proposal to a vote, its decision shall be final, but the Session will in any event give reasons.

The Chair of the meeting will in the meeting advise and assist the proposer so that his proposal is framed in clear terms, is not inconsistent with the Overriding Objective and is in order.

3.8 Means of Public Declaration of Membership

The way that membership is recognised publicly involves one of the three following procedures, but the substance and validity of membership remains the same:

(i) by public profession of faith — for those who have previously been baptised as an infant but have never made a public declaration of their faith before;

(ii) by baptism — for those who have never been baptised (see part 10 of the BCO);

(iii) by resolution of the Session — where an individual has previously been baptised and a member of another church, the Session may resolve to admit an individual to membership. This will be publicly acknowledged in the church notices.

3.8.1 Model Form of Words for Public Declaration of Faith and Membership

The Bible is clear that commitment to, and full involvement in, one congregation of Jesus' universal Church is a basic part of being one of Jesus' followers. As 'members' of Jesus' body, we are to live lives of loving commitment to the family of Christians in one particular church, and of willing submission to the teaching, advice and discipline of the Elders Jesus has placed over that church. Membership of a church, therefore, is simply a normal part of being a Christian.

To become a member of the church, we ask that you affirm your faith in the Holy Trinity through the Lord Jesus Christ, and that you promise to be committed to the church in the way the Bible requires, by answering the questions below:

(i) Do you hold to the Christian Faith in the one God, Father, Son and Holy Spirit, as expressed in the Apostles' Creed?

(ii) Have you been baptised, and have you received from Jesus Christ the cleansing from sin and new life in the Holy Spirit which baptism symbolises?

(iii)   Do you believe that Jesus died on the cross to pay the penalty for your sins, and do you personally repent of your sins and trust in him alone for your forgiveness?

(iv)   Do you recognise the authority of the Elders, and assent to the governance and oversight of the International Presbyterian Church, and are you willing to accept their discipline, if that should ever be necessary?

(v) Do you promise to support this church by prayer, giving money and time, and caring practically for individuals?

(vi)   Do you commit yourself to building and maintaining healthy relationships within this church, treating your fellow believers as your brothers and sisters in Christ?

SECTION 4

DIACONATE

4.1 The Office of Deacon

The Office of Deacon is ordained by Christ for the purpose of ensuring that Christian brotherly love is implemented in practical ways by assisting the needy in the family of the church. It is a separate office from that of Elder (a man may not be both an Elder and a Deacon at the same time). This is, first, because the ministry of mercy to the needy within the church is not to be neglected (Acts 6:1,3). And second, because the ministry of mercy is not to distract the Elders from the ministry of the Word and prayer, which is of first importance (Acts 6:2,4).

Therefore, every IPC congregation shall form and maintain a Diaconate which shall be distinct from the Session while operating in close partnership with and under the supervision of the Session.

The Diaconate is responsible for:

(i)   monitoring the needs of members of the congregation and others who attend regularly;

(ii)   when practical needs (including, but not limited to, financial needs) become evident, taking such steps as may be appropriate to meet those needs from the resources of the congregation (this may include the management and use of specific diaconal funds, as well as organising and directing the church Members to provide practical help when needed);

(iii)   when resources allow, facilitating the church to act in Christian love towards those outside the church in meeting material needs;

(iv)   to do these things in such a way that the Elders are able to concentrate on their God-given ministry of the Word and prayer.

The Diaconate must seek to give effect to the Overriding Objective when it exercises any of its powers or otherwise carries out any of its business.

4.2 Selection, Training, and Appointment

The Session will determine the size the Diaconate in accordance with the size and needs of the congregation and the number of available candidates with the spiritual qualifications for the office.

Deacons shall be ordained by the Session in the manner set out in section 4.6 below and may be either men or women. In all cases, Deacons must be church members in good standing who are in sympathy with the doctrine and practice of the church, particularly the system of doctrine as taught in the Westminster Standards or the Three Forms of Unity.

The Session shall nominate or call for Deacon nominations from the congregation. Nominated candidates shall undertake a period of training and evaluation for the office, including instruction in the Westminster Standards or the Three Forms of Unity, and in understanding the office of Deacon and how it differs from the office of Elder. After such training and evaluation, if it is agreeable to the Session and the candidate, he or she will be presented by the Session to the Congregation for approval by vote at a Members' Meeting.

Deacons shall be ordained (which shall be permanent and only dissoluble for good reason, and only with the permission of the Presbytery). A Deacon or Deaconess may be removed by the Session in similar circumstances as the removal of an Elder as set out in section 5.11 of this BCO.

4.3 Terms of Service

Due to the demands of the service of mercy in diaconal work and the difference in office from that of Elder, the recommended way to ensure sabbatical rest for the Deacons of the church is to use a system of 'terms of service'. Three years would be a reasonable length of term, with re-election possible for subsequent terms. As part of the care of the Diaconate, the Session shall have means of evaluating the Diaconate and individual Deacons. This will include not only the quality of service given, but the effect his or her workload has had on the Deacon's family and spiritual life.

4.4 Relationship to Session

The office of Deacon is one of service. The Diaconate is to assist in the work of administration and service in order that the Elders may more fully devote themselves to the ministry of the Word and prayer.

If a Deacon undertakes confidential business, it shall be kept confidential, except that it should be shared with the Session and the Session only.

The Diaconate must submit its minutes for review by the Session. If it seems to be for the best interest of the church, the Session may require the board of Deacons to reconsider any action, or may, if necessary, overrule it.

Any apparently intractable problem arising between the Diaconate and the Session may be referred by any one Deacon or Elder to Presbytery for assistance in resolution. In the event that any resulting decision of Presbytery is considered erroneous by one or more Elders or Deacons, they may appeal to Synod.

4.5 Organisation of the Diaconate

The Diaconate should organise itself with a chair and secretary who will coordinate the meetings, and see that minutes of all meetings are kept and copied to the Session.

The Diaconate may appoint other Members of the congregation to help in its work but is responsible (under the Session) for the outcome of that work.

The Diaconate is free to manage the work assigned to it by the Session as best seems appropriate, but is at all times under the authority of the Session, which assumes ultimate responsibility for the work and decisions of the Diaconate.

4.6 Ordination of Deacons

1 Timothy 3:8–13 sets forth the scriptural standards for the Diaconate.

When any man or woman shall have been elected to this office, and shall have declared his or her willingness to accept it, he or she shall be ordained in the following manner.

One of the Elders shall state, in a concise manner, the warrant and nature of the office of Deacon, together with the proper character to be sustained, and the duties to be fulfilled by the officer elect; having done this, he shall propose to the candidate in the presence of the congregation, the following questions:

(i)   Do you believe the Scriptures of the Old and New Testaments to be the Word of God, the only infallible rule of faith and practice without error in all matters of which they speak?

(ii)   Are you in sympathy with the understanding of the Scriptures set down in the Westminster Standards or the Three Forms of Unity, and do you approve of the Presbyterian system of Church government?

(iii)   Do you consider yourself, by God's grace, to fulfil the biblical qualifications for Deacons?

(iv)   Will you endeavour not only in your work as Deacon, but in your whole manner of life, to pursue godliness and the fear of the Lord, and to be an example to the church?

(v)   Do you accept the office of Deacon(ess) in this congregation, and promise faithfully to perform all the duties thereof?

(vi)   Do you promise to work for the purity, peace, and unity of the church?

The Deacon elect, having answered these questions in the affirmative, the Elder concerned shall address to the Members of the church the following question:

Do you, the Members of this church, acknowledge and receive this brother/sister as a Deacon(ess), and do you promise to yield to him/her all that honour, encouragement and obedience in the Lord, to which his/her office according to the Word of God, and the constitution of this Church, entitles him/her?

The Session shall then proceed to set apart the candidate, to the office of Deacon, with the laying on of hands and prayer.

SECTION 5

ELDERS

5.1 Role of Elders

Government by Elders is the biblical model of Church government. Presbyterians recognise that this includes the following elements:

(i)   each local church is to be governed by a plurality of Elders;

(ii)   Elders are principally responsible for the welfare of their own congregation, but are also to be involved in the government of the wider Church through the broader councils of the Church;

(iii)   Elders are accountable to the Presbytery of which they are a part;

(iv)   all Elders in a church share responsibility for the ruling of the church, and have parity (equal authority) in this regard. At the same time, within each church there is a distinction in function between Elders who rule (Ruling Elders) and those who both rule and teach (Teaching Elders, also known as Ministers or Pastors) (1 Tim 5:17);

(v)   all Elders should be 'apt to teach' (1 Tim 3:2) so Ruling Elders must be able to do so, while Teaching Elders are charged with the duty of doing so regularly. Similarly, because Word and sacrament are inextricably linked, Ruling Elders may administer the sacraments, while Teaching Elders are charged with the duty of doing so regularly.

5.2 Appointment of Elders

The objective, in appointing Elders in the IPC, shall be to choose and ordain men who will bring glory to our Lord through their life and ministry. As Paul makes clear in the pastoral epistles, the long-term health of the church is critically dependent upon entrusting the oversight of the church and the ministry of the Word to those men, and only those men, who hold to the apostolic gospel, whose lives are exemplary, and who are able to teach the Word of God to the church. The process of assessing a candidate for eldership is to be one which carefully considers his qualifications in these matters.

In accordance with the consistent witness of Scripture to the different roles of men and women in the family and in the Church, and in agreement with the unanimous practice of the worldwide Church until very recent history, Elders in the IPC may only be men.

Given that eldership is about service and sacrifice (Mark 10:43–45; Acts 20:28; 1 Pet 5:1–3), this is neither demeaning to women nor exalting to men, but works for the blessing of all the men, women and children and all relationships within the Church.

The initial evaluation, and if necessary training, of a candidate for the eldership shall generally be the responsibility of the Session in which he would serve. This evaluation shall include opportunity for church Members to register their support or concern with the Session. When the Session is satisfied as to his fitness they shall bring the matter to a vote of the Members of the congregation. It shall be made clear to the congregation that, since the authority to ordain and appoint Elders lies with Presbytery, this is not a final vote on ordination or appointment. Rather it is a vote to request that Presbytery consider him for ordination and/or appointment. This vote shall take place by means of a secret ballot in a Members' Meeting called for the purpose. A three-quarters majority of a quorate meeting is required.

In the case of a new church plant, the role of initial evaluation of a candidate and request to Presbytery for examination will be fulfilled by the Church Planting Committee.

When the need arises, a man may be ordained as an Elder by the Presbytery to serve in another congregation outside the IPC, or to work in an academic institution as a Teacher of Theology or to be a Missionary sent out by the IPC. In such cases, where the prospective Elder will not become part of an IPC Session (known as 'ministering out of bounds'), the initial request for examination will normally come from the Presbytery itself.

A candidate for eldership will be examined by Presbytery for his theological, pastoral and personal fitness according to the biblical standards for eldership. The functions of Presbytery in respect of approval processes may in part or whole be delegated to the Candidates and Credentials' Committee. While the process should avoid unnecessary delay and onerous demands on the candidate, it is appropriate that it should be thorough and rigorous. The details of the examination are set out in the current procedures as approved by Presbytery from time to time.

The assessment procedure for Teaching Elders and Ruling Elders will reflect the parity of the offices and the need for all Elders to be doctrinally orthodox, theologically Reformed, godly in lifestyle and capable as overseers of Christ's people. At the same time, candidates for teaching eldership will be expected, in view of their function as teachers and preachers, to demonstrate a more detailed knowledge of Scripture, grasp of theology and greater ability to teach, than is expected of Ruling Elders.

For Teaching Elders, Presbytery will approve a candidate for ordination by a floor examination and a vote. In the case of ruling Elders, Presbytery may choose to delegate the examination and vote to a commission of the Presbytery.

Once a candidate is approved, he will normally be ordained in the course of a service of worship in the church in which he is to serve. At least two and, if possible, more Members of Presbytery will be present to ordain him with prayer and the laying on of hands.

5.3 Duration of Office

The office of Elder shall be perpetual and subject only to removal for misconduct and other reasons as set out below in section 5.11 and further detailed in section 11.

5.4 Sabbatical Leave

Elders (both ruling and teaching) are encouraged to apply the Sabbath principle in their ministry, by planning sabbatical leave.

5.5 Continuing Education and Training of Others

Every Elder shall seek continually to further his theological or pastoral education and training. He shall also seek opportunities to encourage, mentor and train others less trained or experienced than himself, as assigned by his Session or Presbytery.

5.6 Accountability

Every Elder shall be accountable and answerable to the Session of which he is part and, in particular:

(i)   he shall report to the Session on any matter and in such manner as may be reasonably required by the Session and this shall include all pastoral business;

(ii)   he shall have a duty of self-reporting to the Session, any matter capable of bringing his office into disrepute.

(iii)   he shall have a duty of self referral to Session and Presbytery if at any point, his views or lifestyle change from those he expressed in his ordination vows.

All those ministering out of bounds should be assigned to a Session for accountability and support and should meet with them at regular intervals.

An Elder who remains within the IPC but whose ministry changes significantly in nature should report this to Presbytery for consideration and approval.

5.7 Retirement of an Elder

An Elder may retire by voluntarily relinquishing his responsibilities in his Session and Presbytery, whether this is due to age or other reasons. This shall not annul his office of Elder. A Session shall inform Presbytery as a matter of duty if an Elder retires. The Elder shall then be retired by vote of Presbytery.

A retired Elder may not participate in the business of the Session of which he was a member without the consent of that Session, or their successors, and such consent may be given on any terms and conditions that the Session sees fit to make.

A retired, but not a removed, Elder may participate in Presbytery or Synod Business and shall be considered a Presbytery and Synod Member, but shall not have a vote.

5.8 Transfers of Elders into IPC

An Elder or other ordained officer of a different church may apply to the Presbytery for a transfer of his ordination into the IPC, in which case he shall be examined for his fitness for office in the same manner as men who are examined for ordination.

5.9 Change of Function of Elders from Ruling Elder to Teaching Elder or Vice Versa

An Elder who is functioning as a Ruling Elder may apply to the Presbytery for permission to change his function to that of Teaching Elder, and similarly an Elder who is functioning as a Teaching Elder may apply to the Presbytery for permission to transfer his function to that of Ruling Elder.

A Presbytery Committee shall examine him in accordance with the procedures currently in force and, if satisfied as to his fitness for transferring to the function desired, shall present him to the Presbytery, who shall vote on whether to transfer his status from Ruling to Teaching Elder or vice versa.

5.10 Transfer or Removal of an Elder from IPC

An Elder who ceases to be part of an IPC congregation or whose calling and assignment is no longer with the Presbytery, should request to have his credentials transferred elsewhere or to be removed from Presbytery membership. If this request is not made within a reasonable timescale, Presbytery shall have the authority to remove him.

An Elder wishing to transfer out of the IPC shall give not less than two months' written notice to the Presbytery of his intention to transfer his ordination out of the IPC to another denomination, and particulars of that church shall be given. The Presbytery shall issue a letter of recommendation to that denomination containing a character reference and recommendation, and requesting to be informed when that church has approved him to transfer his ordination to them. When such information is received, the Presbytery shall endorse his certificate of ordination with a memorandum of the transfer and the date upon which it takes effect.

Where an Elder has transferred his ordination out of the IPC to another denomination, the Presbytery may still exercise its powers of removal and dissolution of office but such powers shall not be exercised until the new denomination has had the opportunity of making representations to the Presbytery.

An Elder wishing to transfer out of the IPC is strictly forbidden, while he remains in office as an IPC Elder, from seeking to influence or encourage, whether directly or indirectly, any Member of his congregation to transfer their membership to that or any other church.

5.11 Dissolution of Ordination

5.11.1 Dissolution of Ordination by Elder's Request

An Elder may request the Presbytery to dissolve his ordination and the Presbytery may grant such request, if satisfied that it is appropriate to do so having regard to the Overriding Objective.

5.11.2 Disciplinary Dissolution of Ordination

Please see section 11 for details.

In all cases of dissolution, the Presbytery will make itself (or such other persons as it shall appoint) available for confidential contact with the individual, with the object of achieving reconciliation or resolving any ongoing pastoral problems.

Where an Elder's ordination is dissolved, any Ordination Certificate shall be cancelled and handed back to the Presbytery; the Presbytery shall issue an order to this effect and may give notice of the order to any relevant third party. The congregation over which he held the office of Elder shall be informed of the decision.

5.12 Ordination Certificates, Installation Memoranda and Terms and Conditions

The Presbytery shall issue every Elder with a Certificate of Ordination recording the details of his ordination (including whether he is ordained to the office of Ruling or Teaching Elder) and duly sealed with the Presbytery Seal.

5.13 Remuneration of Elders

Churches should normally pay a stipend or salary to their Teaching Elders and may do so to other staff, as they see fit, having regard to any guidance provided by Presbytery.

5.14 The Ordination of Teaching and Ruling Elders

An ordination (or installation, in the case of a man previously ordained) shall normally take place in the course of a service of worship in the church in which the new Elder is to serve.

The presiding Elder shall report the proceedings of the Presbytery at which this man's call to eldership has been confirmed. He shall then provide a brief explanation of the biblical basis for ordination and impress upon the congregation the significance and gravity of the office, and therefore of what is to follow.

The following form of words shall be used in the ordination of Elders (both Teaching and Ruling):

(i) Do you believe the Scriptures of the Old and New Testaments to be the Word of God, the only infallible rule of faith and practice, without error in all matters of which they speak, including matters of history, the cosmos and ethics?

(ii) Do you sincerely receive and adopt the Westminster Standards (*or* the Three Forms of Unity)[§] as containing the system of doctrine taught in the Holy Scriptures, and setting forth a true understanding of them?

(iii)   Do you believe the Presbyterian form of Church government to be taught in Scripture?

(iv)   Do you promise to submit in the spirit of love to the Session, the Presbytery and Synod as is taught in the Word of God?

(v)   Have you been motivated, as far as you know your own heart, to seek the position of Elder out of love for God and a sincere desire to promote his glory in the gospel of his Son?

(vi)   Do you promise to be faithful and diligent in upholding the truths of the gospel and in maintaining the purity and peace of the Church whatever persecution or opposition you may face as a result?

(vii)   Do you promise to be faithful and diligent in the exercise of all private and personal duties, which are necessary for you as a Christian and as an Elder in Christ's Church? Will you devote yourself to prayer and the study of God's Word, and seek to live your life as an example of Christian discipleship to the flock?

(viii)   Do you promise to be faithful and diligent in the task of leading and ruling the church, seeking to lead the church to greater Christlikeness and further the proclamation and the work of the kingdom of God?

Teaching Elders only:

(ix)   Do you promise to be faithful and diligent in the regular preaching of the Word of God, labouring to proclaim the whole counsel of God faithfully, clearly, consistently, and openly, without fear of the cost to yourself that may result?

(x)   Do you promise to be faithful and diligent in the regular administration of the sacraments in accordance with Christ's commands, and endeavour to communicate their meaning and importance to the church that they may receive them as means of grace?

(This may be omitted in the case of a man being ordained to work as a theologian rather than to minister in a church Session.)

Ruling Elders only:

(ix) Do you promise to proclaim the Word of God faithfully, clearly and openly, and to administer the sacraments in accordance with Christ's commands, without fear of the cost to yourself that may result?

[§ Either the Westminster Standards or the Three Forms of Unity may be used]

The candidate having answered these questions acceptably, the presiding Elder shall ask the members of the congregation the following questions:

(i) Do you, the members of this church, receive (name) as an Elder over this congregation?

(ii) Do you promise to receive teaching from the Word of God from him with meekness and in love?

(iii) Do you promise to give him the honour, encouragement, and obedience in the Lord, to which the office of Elder, according to the Word of God, and the Constitution of this Church, entitles him?

(iv) Do you promise to encourage and assist him in his demanding work, which is for your instruction and Christian growth?

(v)　　　　(In the case of the Teaching Elder only), Do you acknowledge the scriptural requirement that you should provide for your Teaching Elders the financial support that they need?

The people having answered these questions in the affirmative, the presiding Elder shall give the ordination charge, for example, from 2 Timothy 4 or 1 Peter 5, as appropriate.

The candidate shall kneel and the Elders present shall ordain him and install him by the laying on of hands and prayer. (In the case of installation only, he shall be installed with prayer only.)

SECTION 6

SESSION

6.1 Nature of the Session

The Session is the council of the Church, appointed by Presbytery, which is responsible for the government, teaching, pastoral care and discipline of a local congregation. This governing and leading of each church by a plural eldership is established by apostolic authority in Acts 14:23 and described in 1 Peter 5:1–5.

The Session has a duty before Christ to:

(i)   see that the church is taught regularly, faithfully, and clearly from God's Word;

(ii)   gather the church, preferably on the Lord's Day, for corporate worship; and order that worship according to God's Word. This includes the ministry of the Word and sacrament;

(iii)   pastor the flock with a view to their living and growing in Christlikeness;

(iv)   exercise church discipline for the good of the whole family of God;

(v)   devote themselves to the ministry of the Word and prayer;

(vi)   be an example to the flock of godly devotion and lifestyle.

The Session is corporately responsible for the life of the congregation; it has authority to make decisions on behalf of the church and to represent the church to others.

The Session's authority extends to the spiritual and ecclesiastical affairs of the congregation. The administration of such affairs of the congregation in all respects shall be in accordance with the Book of Church Order.

6.2 Composition

A Session shall be composed of at least three Elders [In the Korean Presbytery the requirement shall be at least two Elders]. Should a Session be or become deficient in this regard, a plan and timescale shall be put in place for the appointment of additional Elders. Presbytery shall arrange to provide temporarily another Elder or Elders from another congregation to make up the deficiency. During any periods of time in which this is not possible the Moderator and/or Clerk of Presbytery shall for the time being be acting Elder(s).

6.2.1 Power of Elders to Rule More Than One IPC Congregation, but Only Temporarily

A Session of Elders may govern more than one congregation (and an individual Elder may serve as an Elder in another Session in addition to his own) provided that there is a plan in place for such other congregation to work towards having its own Session within a reasonable time.

6.2.2 Moderator and Clerk

The Pastor (also called the Minister) shall be the moderator of the local Session and shall be answerable to the Presbytery for the teaching of the local congregation. He may from time to time delegate the role of moderating Session meetings.

A Session shall appoint annually one of its members to be the clerk of Session whose function shall include keeping a record of all business conducted, being a contact person for communications with the Presbytery, Synod and others, and seeing that all business is conducted lawfully and in accordance with the Book of Church Order.

6.2.3 Co-option

A man ordained in another Reformed denomination, and retaining his credentials and accountability in his sending Presbytery, may be co-opted by a Session to serve as part of that Session. Such a relationship must be approved by the relevant IPC Presbytery and should only be made as a temporary arrangement for up to three years. After three years, a Session may request that Presbytery allow him to remain for a subsequent period, not exceeding three years. There is no limit to the number of times Presbytery may grant this request, but if the request to extend the relationship is not made after the three years served, his term of service is automatically ended.

A man co-opted onto a Session would not normally be given a vote on that Session. He is not automatically co-opted onto Presbytery; that is a separate decision of Presbytery as described in section 7.5.

6.3 Meetings

6.3.1 Quorum and Mode of Decision-Making

Session meetings must be quorate. In all ruling and decision-making processes, Elders shall have parity.

6.3.2 Mode of Dealing with Dissent and Appeals to the Presbytery

Any Elder, whether present or not, may not later than 14 days after a Session meeting register his dissent to any decision of the Session with the Session clerk and request his dissent and concise reasons to be recorded in the minutes.

A Dissenting Elder may not later than 14 days after he has registered his dissent request the Presbytery to review the decision of the Session by writing a letter to the Presbytery Clerk or Moderator giving his reasons.

The Presbytery Moderator and Clerk shall decide whether to investigate the matter and consider it at the next Presbytery meeting. Should the dissent pertain to the Session to which the Presbytery Moderator or Clerk belong, they shall recuse themselves and appoint another Member of Presbytery to make this decision.

The decision of Presbytery shall be final unless the Dissenting Elder or the Session appeals to the Synod Clerk within 21 days for permission to appeal to the Synod (see Synod Review Board, section 8.5).

Dissenting Elders shall show restraint in discussing with others (and in particular their own congregation) the reasons for their dissent until the matter has been concluded.

6.3.3 Transparency

Sessions may allow observers to attend their meetings, except where either pastoral business or other confidential business is being considered. Minutes shall be made available on request.

Pastoral or other confidential business shall not be recorded in Session minutes, other than by way of discreet outline, but shall be recorded in a confidential minute, which shall remain strictly confidential to the Session and the Presbytery.

6.3.4 Accountability

The Session is corporately accountable and answerable to the Presbytery. The Session shall submit to the authority of the Presbytery subject to a right of appeal to the Synod.

The Session shall report to the Presbytery on any matter as either it shall see necessary or the Presbytery shall require.

6.3.5 Advice by and Instruction from Presbytery

The Session may take advice and instruction on any matter from the Presbytery or any person appointed by the Presbytery for that purpose and the Presbytery may require the Session to take professional advice on a specific matter.

6.4 Church Register

The Session should maintain a Church Register, in the physical form of hardback book(s) written in indelible ink, or computer generated print outs, bound, with each page numbered and signed, containing a historical record of:

(i) People received into membership, including Non-Communing Members;

(ii) Transfers of membership to other churches;

(iii) Instances of church discipline and their resolution;

(iv) Baptisms;

(v) Children approved for participation in the Lord's Supper;

(vi) Solemnisation of Marriages;

(vii) Ordinations to church office, transfers and dissolutions of ordinations;

(viii) Installations and dissolutions of installations;

(ix) Deaths in the congregation and funerals.

In each case, the record shall include the name of the person principally concerned, the names of IPC Elders present, the date and any other relevant information.

The Church Register, provided it is certified by the Session as being true to the best of their knowledge, information and belief as up to a particular date, shall be conclusive evidence of the facts therein set out, although the Session is at liberty to correct errors should it be satisfied such have been made.

Information held on the Church Register shall normally be publicly available.

The Session Clerk shall from time to time supply to the Presbytery Clerk such statistical or other information about membership and other matters in the congregation as he may require.

6.5 Other Duties of the Session

6.5.1 Financial

Sessions shall manage the financial resources of the church in a responsible manner.

Sessions are expected to maintain sufficient funds to meet at least three months regular expenditure of the church at all times.

The Session may delegate the role of treasurer to someone not on the Session but remains responsible for all decisions made. The Session will not normally be involved in management of diaconal funds but remains responsible for them, and so should maintain adequate oversight of the work of the Diaconate.

6.5.2 Safeguarding Children and Vulnerable Groups

Sessions must ensure there is in place an adequate and lawful system for safeguarding children and vulnerable groups.

6.5.3 Employment Laws

Sessions are to ensure they pay appropriate attention to all relevant employment and health and safety laws.

In all cases, the requirement of the Session (or Trustees) to obey secular regulations and laws shall be subject to the Overriding Objective. Advice may be sought from the Presbytery in the first instance when there is a perceived conflict between God's law and secular law, the former always taking precedence.

6.5.4 Trusteeship

Where the local church is a legal entity, Elders shall normally be Trustees (although not all Trustees need be Elders). For this reason, the responsibilities of the members of the Session include all the normal responsibilities of Trustees.

Trustees must seek to give effect to the Overriding Objective when they exercise any of their powers or otherwise carry out any of the church's business.

In the event that the purposes of the Trust are no longer considered viable by the Trustees (for example, if the church has ceased to meet), it is anticipated that the advice and involvement of Presbytery will already have been sought, but in any event, at that point the Trustees shall be obliged to take the advice of Presbytery in the matter of asset disbursement. In this situation, alongside any statutory requirements for winding up the Trust, Trustees should ensure employees are paid appropriate redundancy pay, all debts are settled, and any residual property or assets shall then be transferred to the body which shall most closely perpetuate the original purpose of the Trust. The *cy près doctrine* shall apply in favour of the Presbytery, if there is no more logical inheritor. If a local church Trust is being wound up, it may not disburse any asset to a third party without consultation with Presbytery.

SECTION 7

PRESBYTERY

7.1 Principles

The Presbytery is the council of the Church which provides oversight, accountability and encouragement to congregations within a specific geographical area and the Elders who oversee them. As such, it is responsible for nurturing the spiritual life of churches under its care, for promoting and planning the establishment of new churches, and equipping and encouraging Elders in their ministry. As a court, Presbytery examines, ordains, admits, removes and disciplines Elders. It determines doctrinal and pastoral issues arising from its churches. It has the power to organise, receive, combine and dissolve congregations. It is responsible for oversight of men training for eldership. It has a responsibility to provide gospel resources to the wider Church.

7.2 General Powers and Responsibilities of the Presbytery

The Presbytery is required to seek to give effect to the Overriding Objective when it exercises any power or otherwise carries out any business.

The Presbytery shall have the following general powers:

(i)   To receive and consider appeals, complaints, and references brought before it in an orderly manner;

(ii)   To assume jurisdiction in cases in which the Session cannot exercise its authority, or where there is no Session;

(iii)   To receive under its care, to train and to examine candidates for the ministry;

(iv)   To receive, ordain, install, censure and dismiss Elders;

(v)   To review the records of church Sessions, to ensure that they observe the provisions of this Book of Church Order and the Constitution of the church;

(vi)   To see that the lawful injunctions of the Synod are obeyed;

(vii)   To condemn erroneous opinions which injure the purity or peace of the Church; to visit churches for the purpose of inquiring into and redressing the evils that may have arisen in them; to unite or divide churches; to form and receive new churches; to take special oversight of churches without Teaching Elders; to dissolve churches; to dismiss churches with their consent;

(viii)   To devise measures for the enlargement of the Church within its bounds;

(ix)   To order whatever pertains to the spiritual welfare of the churches under its care;

(x)   To establish itself as a legal entity for the better administration of its business and for furtherance of its objectives;

(xi)   To purchase, lease, let, mortgage, charge, licence and generally manage and deal with any property (whether movable or immovable);

(xii)   To delegate all or any of its powers to any person or committee or commission and to define their remit;

(xiii)   To pay for professional services including when provided by Members of Presbytery;

(xiv)   To propose to the Synod such measures as may be of common advantage to the Church at large;

(xv)   To form a seminary or any other educational establishment and transfer funds thereto;

(xvi)   The Presbytery shall take care to order its financial business according to the Word of God and national legal requirements (so far as the Word of God allows);

(xvii)   The Presbytery shall not possess or acquire any monetary or financial assets including property from a local congregation, unless the congregation chooses to bequeath those assets to the Presbytery. In the event the Presbytery uses its powers to dissolve a congregation, the assets of the congregation remain with the church and would not be subject to seizure by Presbytery.

7.3 Autonomy and Duty of Referral

A Presbytery shall have autonomy of authority over all matters within its charge (assuming conformity to the Overriding Objective), with the exception of the duty of referral.

A Presbytery has a duty of referral to Synod in three situations in which it is not competent to act independently:

(i) When the matter under consideration has an impact or is likely to have an impact on other Presbyteries or the IPC as a whole.

(ii) When the matter under consideration requires or implies a change to the confessional standards, the constitution of the IPC, or to the Book of Church Order.

(iii) When the matter under consideration may imply a significant change to hitherto accepted IPC doctrine and practice.

In the event that a Presbytery makes referral of an issue to the Synod, the status quo shall apply until the matter has been ruled on by Synod.

Presbyteries shall not interfere with one another's business. Disputes between Presbyteries must be referred to Synod.

7.4 Membership

Presbytery consists of all members of constituent Sessions who are ordained in the IPC, and other men ordained as

Teaching Elders and authorised by Presbytery to work out of bounds such as Church Planters, Teachers of Theology and Missionaries sent out by the IPC or serving in non-IPC churches.

Voting in Presbytery is restricted to all Teaching Elders and two Ruling Elders from each congregation with up to 100 members and another Ruling Elder for each additional 100 members (or part thereof). These shall be nominated by each church Session, the names being submitted to the Clerk in advance of each Presbytery meeting. In all decision-making processes, Presbytery Elders shall have parity.

The authority of Presbytery does not derive from the Sessions under its care but from Christ, and therefore a Presbytery has its own intrinsic authority.

7.5 Co-option

Presbytery shall have the capacity to co-opt as non-voting members men already ordained in other denominations in the following instances:

(i)   Teaching Elders — working in an IPC church or church plant or out of bounds;

(ii)   Ruling Elders — such as those who have previously served in local congregations who may be drawn in for their wisdom and association with the work of IPC;

(iii)   Missionaries sent from other denominations to work with the IPC.

In each case, the agreement of the individual, and the receiving and sending organisations (where applicable) shall be required. Moreover he must maintain his credentials, and therefore his accountability, with the Presbytery by which he has been sent. If he does not have such a relationship with a sending Presbytery, then he should apply to transfer his ordination to the IPC and thereby become a full (voting) member of Presbytery.

7.6 Officers

The officers of the Presbytery shall be the Moderator and the Clerk. These are to be elected every year.

7.6.1 Appointment and Function of Moderator (or Chairman)

The Presbytery shall appoint annually one of their number to be their Moderator whose function shall include:

(i)   convening Presbytery meetings;

(ii)   determining the business to be brought before the Presbytery;

(iii)   conducting and presiding over all Presbytery business.

The Presbytery may resolve to allow the Moderator appropriate expenses and a stipend as it sees fit.

7.6.2 Appointment and Function of Presbytery Clerk

The Presbytery shall appoint annually one of their number to be their Clerk whose functions shall include:

(i)   the dissemination of an agenda in consultation with the Moderator a minimum of two weeks in advance of Presbytery;

(ii)   keeping minutes of all business conducted;

(iii)   being a contact person for communications with Synod, Presbytery members, Sessions and others;

(iv)   seeing that all business is conducted lawfully and in accordance with the Book of Church Order;

(v)   making the practical arrangements for the holding of Presbytery meetings and any worship service of the Presbytery.

The Presbytery may resolve to allow the Clerk appropriate expenses and a stipend as it sees fit.

7.7 Meetings and Procedures

7.7.1 Ordinary Meetings

The Presbytery shall meet not less than twice per year at such times and venues as the Moderator shall decide.

The dates and venues for these meetings shall be notified to all Members of the Presbytery a minimum of 8 weeks beforehand.

7.7.2 Extraordinary Meetings

The Moderator may call an Extraordinary Meeting at the request or with the concurrence of one Teaching Elder and two other Elders from at least two different churches. Should the Moderator be for any reason unable to act, the Presbytery Clerk shall, under the same requirements, issue the call. If both Moderator and Presbytery Clerk are unable or unwilling to act, any two Teaching Elders and two ruling Elders of at least three different churches shall have power to call a meeting.

Notice of the special meeting shall be sent to Presbytery members not less than ten days in advance. In the notice, the purpose of the meeting shall be stated, and no business other than that named in the notice is to be transacted.

The Presbytery shall also convene an Extraordinary Meeting when directed to do so by the Synod for the transaction of designated business only.

7.7.3 Presbytery Committee of Enquiry (PCE)

From time to time between Presbytery meetings there may be a need for Presbytery to act with urgency regarding matters of concern brought to its officers.

A presbytery committee of enquiry may be formed by the Moderator of Presbytery with the agreement of the Clerk of Presbytery when a matter concerning the church or its member(s) has been brought before the Presbytery Moderator and Clerk, consideration of which in their judgement:

a.   may be a matter which is the proper business of Presbytery and

b.   cannot wait until the next scheduled meeting of Presbytery and

c.   does not, at initial assessment, justify an extraordinary meeting of Presbytery.

A PCE shall have specified terms of reference drawn up by the Moderator and Clerk of Presbytery in respect of the issue at hand.

7.7.3.1 Composition of a PCE

A PCE shall be composed of the Moderator of Presbytery (or their deputized nominee), the Clerk of Presbytery (or their deputized nominee) and three other Elders called by the Moderator to participate (giving due regard to the need to avoid conflicts of interest). Any potential member of the PCE who has a conflict of interest or direct involvement on the issue at hand shall recuse themselves from participation.

7.7.3.2 Principles of a PCE

A PCE shall undertake its work with the following principles in mind:

a.   It is primarily for fact finding purposes

b.   It shall undertake all its activities with the primary purpose of fulfilling the overriding objective. It shall seek the peace and harmony of the church.

c.   It shall seek honest perspectives and accounts of all involved in the issue at hand before reaching any conclusions or recommendations.

d.   It shall undertake to communicate clearly the progress of the enquiry to all parties concerned, specifically when decisions are reached or reports made.

e.   It shall maintain a pastoral awareness of all parties involved in the matter at hand.

f.   Although it may make recommendations to Presbytery it is specifically not a decision making nor disciplinary body of the church.

g.   It shall abide by the principles of confidentiality set out below.

A PCE shall nominate a chair and note keeper from amongst its membership. The chair shall be responsible for making arrangements for meetings and timely conduct of the enquiry. The chair shall be responsible for collating the final report of the committee to Presbytery.

A PCE shall anticipate the full cooperation of all church members in discharging its duties.

Where matters of a personal nature are concerned those contributing to the PCE shall be expected to refrain from discussing the issue further than those already involved during the period of the enquiry.

7.7.3.3 Procedure for PCE

The procedure followed by the PCE shall necessarily be dependent upon the particular circumstances of the issue at hand but shall generally be expected to involve the following steps:

1)   Fact finding
- The members of the PCE may delegate aspects of this stage to a small subgroup of not less than 2 of their number (for instance determined by those living more conveniently to access those involved in the issue at hand).

- The PCE shall make arrangements to gather written and preferably face to face accounts from those directly involved in the issue at hand. Each individual contributing to the enquiry shall have the terms of reference available to them before hand and shall be able to be accompanied by a trusted friend if they so choose to any meetings. There shall be no legal representative at any PCE meeting, this being a non-disciplinary process.

2)   Review

The members of the PCE shall meet to discuss and review their findings and prayerfully consider the options. It may be appropriate to undertake one or several of the following at this stage:
- Clarify aspects of discussions or written submissions with those who made them
- Meet individuals for further discussion or for pastoral care
- Meet with particular groups (for example the Session or Congregation of a church)
- Offer appropriate pastoral support to those involved in the issue at hand

3)   Report

The PCE shall write a report and make recommendations.
- Any individual upon whom the report or a recommendation therein will have direct impact shall have a right to see the draft report and make request to correct factual inaccuracy but not the opinion of the PCE contained in the report. The PCE may accept or reject such a correction of fact, giving reasons.
- Any individual concerned (whether a member of the PCE or not) may dissent from or assent to the report of the PCE. Any dissent(s) shall be appended in written form to the report.

- The report shall usually be presented at the next Presbytery (in open or if necessary when there are matters of a personal nature, in closed session) however if the PCE determine that the matter cannot wait then they shall have the ability to call an extraordinary meeting of Presbytery (in accordance with the BCO) for the report on the issue at hand to be considered.
- Subsequent to the deliverance of a report to Presbytery, the work of a PCE shall be considered to be concluded unless Presbytery determines there are further matters requiring an extension to the PCE.

7.7.3.4 Outcomes of a PCE

The report of a PCE will usually contain some recommendations to Presbytery for its consideration. A PCE (or its individual members) does not have autonomous authority to act for Presbytery (which would require a Commission to be formed) and therefore is not expected to make recommendations to churches or individuals.

Recommendations may include one or more of the following:

1.   Finding of 'no case to answer'
2.   Recommendation to commend for action or lack of action
3.   Recommendation to censure for an action or lack of action
4.   Recommendation to accept a resignation or period of sabbatical
5.   Recommendation to institute formal disciplinary action (see section on Discipline)
6.   Recommendation for further investigations by PCE
7.   Recommendation to institute a Commission of Presbytery

8.   Recommendation to institute additional support to a given situation

7.7.3.5 Principles for handling information disclosed to members of the PCE

In the context of a PCE the disclosure of sensitive and personal information is possible. It is important that the person who is sharing or disclosing personal information has confidence that what is said will not be indiscriminately spread to others.   PCE members must be trustworthy in dealing with personal matters to enable people to open up with real confidence.

Members of a PCE shall therefore abide by the following principles:

a.   Each PCE member has a responsibility to handle potentially personal information sensitively, at all times.   It might be right to share knowledge but this must only be done after a period of reflection to ensure that the disclosure is appropriate and done with the best intent to build up rather than tear down.

b.   There are important occasions when we must pass information on. Yet even then the information needs to be passed on in the right way, at the right time and to the right people:
•   Child protection issues: if there is a concern regarding child protection or protection of a vulnerable adult, this must be taken to the designated child protection team for a given church and/or the proper legal authorities. This is a legal obligation.
•   Concern for the health and/or safety of someone in the Church

c.   As Presbyterians we believe that situations in churches are best dealt with by the combined wisdom of a number of church elders. Therefore anyone disclosing information to an elder should always understand that it may be appropriate and or necessary to share this with other elders in the PCE, the Session or the Presbytery. At the same time it is a duty of elders to handle such information wisely and not discuss it with others where it is neither appropriate nor necessary. Decisions over what should be disclosed are therefore based upon trust rather than unqualified promises of confidentiality, which may unhelpfully bind consciences.

d.   Sharing our problems and concerns with each other is central to supporting one another both in prayer and in practical ways yet just as there is the potential for great help being given there is also potential for great hurt being received in matters of a sensitive nature. We all need to think very carefully before discussing someone else's problems.   Proverbs 18:6 tells us: The words of a whisperer are like delicious morsels; they go down to the inner parts of the body. Gossip is tempting and inherently interesting to us. We need to be on our guard to avoid it.

e.   The gospel of Jesus Christ is not afraid to bring matters into the open in an appropriate way. Openness can often be the very things that sets us free from the fear of being discovered or known. Appropriate openness is often the thing which assures us that, as believers, we are already fully, perfectly known and fully and perfectly loved and accepted through Jesus Christ our Lord.

In summary this is what a church member can expect from the PCE:

• To take very seriously the bible's teaching not to be a tale-bearer, not to engage in gossip, idle speculations or spread rumours.

• To take seriously the call to shepherd the flock of God. The overiding aim of the PCE is to honour God and build up his church whilst being redemptive and helpful to everyone.

• In the case of elders who are married it is recognised that they may wish to share some of what they are told with their wives to allow the sharing of burdens that is essential to a fruitful Christian marriage. Taking that into account, however, discretion will be shown by the elder in deciding what is appropriate to disclose to his wife with reference to the particular situation he is facing. His wife is also bound to follow these guidelines on confidentiality to the same full extent as her husband. The PCE, as elders of the IPC, must commit themselves, along with their wives, to serving the church family with integrity and to earn and guard the trust of the church family in doing so.

• To be able to share with fellow elders anything that is discussed. This openness between elders is for the protection of the church. The elders have been set apart by the church to lead the body and they must be united in order to fulfill this calling effectively. If information is shared with an elder that may pose a potential threat to the welfare of any part of the church it is vital that they consult with fellow elders about such matters.

• The outcome (usually a report) of a PCE will be discussed at Presbytery but this will be in closed session (only Presbytery members will be present) if there are sensitive personal matters involved. The same principled described here will be respected by all Presbytery members in this situation.

• If the PCE decides that the welfare of the individual or others is at stake then it may be their duty to share information with the appropriate authorities (civil, family or church). This is for the protection of the individual and the church. The PCE would endeavour first to secure an individual's agreement to make the necessary disclosure themselves if at all possible. This could, in some circumstances mean speaking with police, legal courts, parents or spouses about matters discussed.

• Presbytery may decide to involve others outside of Presbytery as sources of help.

• The PCE will be glad to discuss these principles with members further at any time.

In turn, Church members are asked to act with discretion in respect of matters considered by a PCE and where necessary to bring their concerns to the PCE.

7.8 Transparency

Presbytery is an open meeting and observers are welcome. Presbytery shall have the power to meet in closed session when the nature of the business requires it.

Pastoral or other confidential business shall not be recorded in minutes, other than by way of discreet outline, but shall be recorded in confidential minutes which shall remain strictly confidential to the Presbytery, except that Synod may request to see confidential minutes if the need arises.

7.9 Reporting

The Presbytery shall keep a full and accurate record of its proceedings, and shall provide them to the Synod for review. It shall report to the Synod important changes such as ordinations, the union and the division of churches, and the formation of new ones.

7.10 Conflict of Interest

The work of the Presbytery shall be administered by each Elder in his capacity as an individual Presbytery Member and not in his capacity as Session Member working corporately within a Session. It shall be presumed unless it is proved to the contrary in any particular situation (for example, in a situation involving an individual Elder's legal duties as Trustee) that no significant conflict of interest arises between these two capacities. Accordingly, each Presbytery Member shall be free as far as possible to bring to the Presbytery an objective appraisal of the work and needs of his own Session as well as his own congregation.

An Elder who perceives a potential or definite conflict of interest shall be duty bound to raise this matter at the outset of the relevant item of business or as soon thereafter as it becomes apparent. Where an issue is raised about whether there is a conflict of interest, that issue shall be resolved by the Presbytery Moderator who shall give directions on how that Elder should proceed.

7.11 Dissent

Any Elder, whether present or not, voting or not, may, not later than 14 days after a Presbytery meeting, register his dissent to any decision of the Presbytery by writing a letter to the Presbytery Clerk explaining his dissent with concise reasons, which will then be added to the minutes of the meeting (such an Elder is referred to as 'a Dissenting Elder').

A Dissenting Elder may, not later than 14 days after he has registered his dissent, appeal to the Synod to review the decision of the Presbytery by writing a letter to the Moderator or Clerk of Synod expressing his full reasoning (see section 8.5).

Dissenting Elders shall show restraint in discussing with others the reasons for their dissent until the matter has been concluded.

SECTION 8

SYNOD

8.1 Principles

The Synod shall seek to advance the worship, edification, and witness of the whole Church. It shall determine all doctrinal and disciplinary questions brought before it from the more local councils as a final court of appeal. It shall constitute the bond of union, peace, love, and mutual confidence among all our churches.

The deliverances of the Synod are to be received with deference and submission, not only because of their fidelity to the Word of God, but also because of the nature of the Synod as the supreme council of the Church.

The Synod shall determine the boundaries of each Presbytery and oversee their operation. The Synod shall have the authority to recognise and to dissolve Presbyteries within its bounds.

The Synod is the competent body to manage relationships with other Church bodies or organisations. The Synod shall aim to cooperate with other orthodox Christian Synods and church groupings, seeking the peace and unity of the Church to the greatest degree possible. Where appropriate (and particularly with other Presbyterian denominations) fraternal relations shall be established and warmly maintained, through regular exchange of news, mutual encouragement, mutual prayer and fellowship together.

The Synod shall take care to order its financial business according to the Word of God and national legal requirements (so far as the Word of God allows).

8.2 Membership

The Synod of this Church shall consist of all Elders who are members of constituent Presbyteries.

Voting is restricted to voting members of Presbyteries. Voting members means all Teaching Elders who may vote at presbytery and two Ruling Elders from each congregation with up to 100 Members and another Ruling Elder for each additional 100 Members or part thereof. All voting elders shall be notified to the Synod Clerk in advance of Synod by the clerk of their Presbytery.

8.3 Officers

The officers of the Synod shall be the Moderator and the Clerk. These are to be elected every year and should preferably come from different Presbyteries.

8.3.1 Appointment and Function of Moderator

The Synod shall elect annually one of their number to be its

Moderator, whose function shall include (in addition to any other function designated by the Synod):

(i)   convening Synod meetings;

(ii)   determining the business to be brought before the Synod;

(iii)   conducting and presiding over all Synod business.

The Synod may resolve to allow the Moderator appropriate expenses and a stipend as it sees fit.

8.3.2 Appointment and Function of Synod Clerk

The Synod shall elect annually one of their number to be its Clerk, whose function shall include:

(i)   the dissemination of an agenda in consultation with the Moderator a minimum of two weeks in advance of Synod;

(ii)   keeping minutes of all business conducted;

(iii)   being a contact person for communications with the Presbytery Officers, Synod members and others;

(iv)   seeing that all business is conducted lawfully and in accordance with the Book of Church Order;

(v)   making the practical arrangements for the holding of Synod meetings and any worship service of the Synod.

The Synod may resolve to allow the Clerk appropriate

expenses and a stipend as it sees fit.

8.4 Meetings

8.4.1 Ordinary Meetings

The Synod shall meet not less than once per year at such times and venues as the Moderator shall decide.

The business of Synod shall be determined by the Moderator and Clerk with regard to any matters raised by constituent Presbyteries.

The agenda, including any late business, must be adopted by Synod at the beginning of the business of the meeting.

The dates and venues for these meetings shall be notified to all members of constituent Presbyteries a minimum of 8 weeks beforehand.

8.4.2 Extraordinary Meetings

The Moderator shall call an Extraordinary Meeting at the request or with the concurrence of at least one Presbytery Moderator or at least two Elders from two Presbyteries. Should the Synod Moderator be for any reason unable to act, the Synod Clerk shall, under the same requirements, issue the call. If both Moderator and Synod Clerk are unable to act, a minimum of one Presbytery Moderator and two other Elders representing at least two Presbyteries shall have power to call a meeting.

Notice of the Extraordinary Meeting shall be sent to all

Synod members not less than 21 days in advance to each member of constituent Presbyteries. In the notice, the purpose of the meeting shall be stated, and no business other than that named in the notice is to be transacted.

8.5 Appeals — The Review Board

Synod shall have the authority, but not the obligation, to review any matter that has been decided by a more local council of the church where an appeal has been made to Synod.

When an appeal is brought to the attention of the Moderator or Clerk, they shall determine that it is in order:

(i) That it is clearly stated and submitted within the appropriate time frame.

(ii) That the matter has been duly considered and ruled on by the appropriate Presbytery.

The Synod Clerk and Moderator shall have power to form an ad hoc committee, the 'Review Board' of four members comprising the Synod Moderator, the Synod Clerk, one Teaching Elder and one Ruling Elder (the latter two where possible drawn from a Presbytery other than the subject of the appeal). If a Review Board member recognises that he has a potential or real conflict of interest, he shall recuse himself and an alternate member shall then be sought.

The Review Board so formed shall have delegated authority to consider the appeal brought to Synod.

The Review Board may decide:

1.   Not to hear the appeal

If the Review Board considers the matter to be vexatious, it may decide not to hear the appeal. The matter is concluded and the original Presbytery decision stands. There is no further avenue of appeal. The Review Board shall issue this decision to the appellant within one calendar month of receiving the appeal.

2.   To hear the appeal

If the Review Board decides to hear the appeal, it shall meet in closed session as soon as practicable to consider the matter and has authority to inspect any record of any Church council pertaining to the issue and to call any Member of the church who might have knowledge of the matter. In all cases, the Moderator of the respective Presbytery and the appellant shall be afforded the opportunity to speak to the Review Board.

The Synod Clerk shall keep a minute of any meetings and a record of decisions of Review Boards. These minutes shall be kept as notes apart and are not available for public scrutiny, except when so requested by Synod.

The Review Board decision may take one of three forms:

(i) That the decision of Presbytery is upheld. This decision is final. There is no further avenue of appeal.

(ii)   That the decision of Presbytery should be modified in some specified way. This decision of the Review Board shall be subject to the approval of the next full meeting of Synod.

(iii)   That the matter is of sufficient gravity for it to be brought to a full meeting of Synod. The Review Board shall refrain from giving a decision in this case.

Upon reaching a decision the work of a given Review Board is complete and it shall be disbanded.

The Synod Clerk shall make a report of any Review Board activities to the next full meeting of Synod. Synod has the authority to reconsider any decision of a Review Board.

The decision of a full meeting of Synod is final.

8.6 Review of Presbytery Business

Synod shall have an annual responsibility to review the business of Presbyteries within its charge.

This shall usually take the form of a written and verbal report to Synod by the Moderators of Presbyteries.

Synod shall have authority to call for and inspect the records of Presbyteries within its charge.

8.7 Matters of Significant Change

Any change to the subordinate standards, the Constitution or the Book of Church Order of the International Presbyterian Church is a matter of significant change and is the proper business of the Synod. Presbyteries may suggest or request such changes but do not have the power to implement them.

In considering any such change, Synod shall have a primary obligation to uphold the Overriding Objective and maintain submission to the Holy Scriptures and the subordinate standards.

If the Synod considers a Presbytery has acted *ultra vires* (beyond its power), then Synod shall have authority to call the matter before it. The status quo shall then pertain until Synod has ruled on the matter in question.

8.8 Transparency

Synod is an open meeting and observers are welcome. Synod shall have the power to meet in closed session when the nature of the business requires it.

Pastoral or other confidential business shall not be recorded in minutes, other than by way of discreet outline, but shall be recorded in a confidential minute which shall remain strictly confidential to the Synod.

8.9 The establishment of a Presbytery

The establishment, dissolution or merging of Presbyteries shall be a recorded decision of Synod and is designated as Special Business in line with Section 2.2 of the BCO.
A request for establishment of full Presbytery status shall be by motion of a Proto-presbytery and shall also require:
a. The existence of five established churches for minimum of 1 year within the Proto-presbytery
b. Adoption by the proto-Presbytery of the BCO in its latest version approved by Synod as the valid law of the Church (and in the case of a non-English speaking Proto-presbytery, to have a full translation available).

8.10 The dis-establishment of a Presbytery

A Presbytery whose number of established churches falls below the specified minimum (see section 8.9) should:

i) notify Synod Moderator and Clerk of the situation.
ii) submit a plan for recovery within 2 years.
iii) Synod should consider a move to proto-Presbytery status or a merger with another Presbytery if the Presbytery remains in the same situation for more than 2 years.

SECTION 9

CHURCH OVERSIGHT

It is the cheerful responsibility of a Presbytery to operate meaningful oversight of the churches in its care. This oversight should seek to endorse good practice, counsel in making plans, support through times of difficulty and maintain a lively relationship of Presbytery with the churches under its care. It shall be effected on an ongoing basis by the regular exchange of news, the meeting together in Presbytery and Synod, the reports of Sessions to Presbytery and through ad hoc visits and inspection of records.

Aspects of church oversight may be delegated to a Church Planting Committee of Presbytery.

9.1 Church Planting Committee (or Equivalent)

The Presbytery or its delegated Church Planting Committee shall initiate and oversee all steps involving the planting, nurture and particularising of an IPC congregation. No step shall be taken by the Presbytery which is against the wishes of the Synod, and all steps which are taken shall so far as possible include involvement of and consultation with a congregation which is reasonably local to the church plant.

Such steps in relation to IPC church planters shall ordinarily include:

(i) the recruitment and training of potential church planters for IPC churches;

(ii) the consideration and approval of church planting proposals with a view to the suitability of the church planter, the adequacy of the funding available and the potential (as far as may be discerned) of the new church to grow to self-sufficiency in a reasonable time frame;

(iii) the appointment and commissioning of church planters with specific missions over a specific time period;

(iv) where a church planter is new to the IPC and/or not yet ordained, recommending him to the Candidates and Credentials Committee for assessment;

(v) arranging prayer and pastoral support during such time period;

(vi) providing advice regarding fundraising, and administering any funds the Presbytery may have available for church planting;

(vii)   assessing the growth and health of a church plant and its prognosis;

(viii)   dealing with the transitional stages for bringing a church plant into a fully fledged particularised IPC church, including all its legal requirements such as charity registration;

(ix) winding up the church plant if it is not viable and

learning lessons, while seeking to nurture any hurting relationships and bring about reconciliation where necessary.

The Presbytery shall so far as possible encourage and review, and, if necessary, give directions for the planting of a daughter congregation by a local congregation.

There are four recognised stages by which a church plant moves from being a proposal to a particularised church.

Stage 1: Proposal

The Church Planting Committee is considering whether to take a church plant under care of Presbytery. In principle, the IPC will seek to adopt plants that have a reasonable chance of being both Presbyterian and a functioning church.

There is no commitment from the Presbytery to oversee a plant, and no commitment from the IPC to adopt the plant if it is established. No formal accountability exists to the IPC but non-financial support might be offered.

Examples include:

(i)   a church planter has not yet begun their work;

(ii) an established Church is considering whether the IPC is the right denomination for them.

Those involved in this work shall be made welcome to open sessions of Presbytery business.

Stage 2: Church Plant

Once a proposal has been approved and the gathering phase starts, the project formally becomes an IPC church plant.

In order for a proposal to become a church plant, the proposal must have been approved by the Presbytery. In particular, due diligence of the Church Planting Committee (or equivalent) shall include:

(i)   taking up independent references;

(ii)   an assessment of how ready the planter's family is for the process of church planting, being sure that the planter's wife is aware of what is likely to be involved in church planting, and that they have discussed what their ministry together will look like;

(iii)   an assessment of need, doing our best to ensure that we are not planting unnecessarily close to good local evangelical churches;

(iv)   an assessment of budget, what support is likely to be needed and what sources of support are being looked into;

(v)   an assessment of what training or relevant experience the church planter has or might need.

A church plant comes under the care of the Church Planting Committee, and the church planter is expected to give regular reports to the committee.

The church planter must have been approved by Presbytery to be a Teaching Elder. Formal approval of a plant may come some time before the planter is in situ so that they can have the status of an approved proposal. This may be helpful as they seek funding, so that they can make it clear that they have IPC endorsement and commitment.

Stage 3: Mission church

Mission status allows there to be a small functioning church, albeit one that needs significant oversight. A mission church can receive Members and administer the sacraments.

In order for a church plant to become a mission church:

(i)   There must be regular Sunday services.

(ii) There needs to be a core of people who are committed to the church plant.

(iii) The move to mission status must be approved by Presbytery.

Given that the timing of Presbytery may not fit well with when it is appropriate for a church to start administering the sacraments, the Moderator of Presbytery has delegated authority to grant provisional approval for the move to mission church status, in the expectation that this will be approved at the next Presbytery.

A mission church is under care of the Church Planting Committee and the church planter is expected to give regular reports to the committee.

Stage 4: Established Church

A local church is recognised to be 'established' (this is used to mean the same thing as historically meant by 'particularised') when it has developed to the point that it no longer needs the oversight of the Church Planting Committee. It is therefore directly accountable to Presbytery through the usual channels.

In order for a mission church to be recognised as 'established', it must have:

(i)   at least three Elders[2], preferably on site;

(ii) regular meetings with at least 15 Members in good standing — it is expected that these members should be contributing financially to the church;

(iii) a significant proportion of the church's financial obligations (around at least 50%) being met by congregational giving;

(iv) Presbytery will then assess the general health of the church and approve the move to established church status.

If a church loses its Elders or a group of its Members so that it goes below the thresholds, it will have an 18-month time frame to rebuild before being moved to mission church status. This change will be noted in the minutes of Presbytery. It is a requirement of Presbytery that churches will communicate a change of status to Presbytery.

Presbytery shall keep a current list of established churches,

---

[2] [at least two Elders in the Korean Presbytery]

mission churches and approved church plants.

9.2 Appointment of Presbytery Elders to a Session

Where the need arises, an Elder or Elders of one IPC congregation may be appointed by the Presbytery (following consultation with the relevant congregation) to serve any other congregation, whether in the IPC or not, in which case such appointment shall be on an interim basis only for a period not exceeding 12 months, but the Presbytery may for good and sufficient reason extend such time by such further period or periods as may be appropriate, but not exceeding three years in all from the date of the original appointment.

In the case of mission churches this should only be used rarely. When a church is not able to raise up leaders, this is usually a sign that there are problems with the health of the church. Moreover, a borrowed Elder will struggle to know the congregation well and provide oversight. There are situations where this can be beneficial, but it ought not to be the norm that a church moves to being a particularised church on the strength of having a borrowed Elder as one of its two Elders.

9.3 The Winding up of an IPC Church Plant

Presbytery (through its Church Planting Committee) may recognise that a church plant is not making progress towards mission church status and is unlikely to do so. In this circumstance, Presbytery may direct that a church plant is wound up. Presbytery shall take all possible steps to offer support and reconciliation to those involved and to learn lessons therefrom.

9.4 Admission of a Congregation to the IPC

The Presbytery may receive into its care a congregation wishing to become an IPC congregation either for fully organised status or mission status ('the New Congregation') provided that:

(i)   all of the Elders or other leaders of that congregation are IPC Elders or have transferred their ordinations into IPC according to the method set out in the BCO;

(ii)   the Presbytery is satisfied that at least two thirds of people in the New Congregation consent to becoming IPC Members.

Upon such joining, the Presbytery Clerk shall take such steps as may be appropriate to ensure that the New Congregation:

(i)   identifies itself by name or otherwise as an IPC church;

(ii)   complies with all relevant legal requirements for entry into the IPC;

(iii)   recognises the primacy of the BCO and any subsequent amendments agreed at Synod in determining the affairs of the congregation. This recognition should be explicit in any governing documents held or adopted at a local level.

(iv)   Upholds the Overriding Objective.

9.5 Breakdown of Relationships

A Presbytery may become aware that a congregation within its bounds has fallen on troubled times, indicated by marked fall-off in attendances at public worship, reduction in contributions to church funds, alienation of office bearers and such like. In these cases it is the duty of the Presbytery to take action to try to resolve difficulties and to restore harmony and the general health of the congregation.

Exceptionally, as it makes these efforts, Presbytery may become convinced that there is a breakdown in relations within a Session or congregation, not involving moral delinquency of any sort, but due to certain incompatibilities of temperament. In that case, and after prolonged effort to resolve the situation, Presbytery has authority to issue discipline as it sees fit, including but not limited to releasing the Teaching Elder from his charge.

9.6 Effecting a Separation of a Congregation from IPC

While the IPC is desirous to maintain harmonious relationships with its constituent churches, it is recognised that there is a possibility that, as we seek to welcome congregations and new members into our fellowship, members and exceptionally congregations may grow apart from the denomination. We therefore recognise the following mechanism to permit separation of a congregation (which is defined as the express desire of more than three quarters of the membership of a congregation to leave the denomination; a smaller group leaving the denomination shall not constitute separation and would not initiate this process but will be cause for Presbytery's involvement and support for a local church).

Separation may be initiated by the Presbytery or by a Session. It is presumed and envisaged that this would mark the end point of sincere dialogue and effort to reconcile the congregation within the denomination.

The intention to separate must be intimated in writing to the Presbytery Clerk and Moderator by the Clerk of Session of the congregation (or another Elder) giving clear reasons for the decision and indicating that the congregation has voted by three-quarters majority at a quorate meeting so to do. It should be noted that this process should not be initiated if an Elder from the congregation is undergoing a disciplinary process.

Upon receipt of the intention to separate letter, Presbytery shall appoint a liaison officer (usually the Clerk) to facilitate the process. The Presbytery (or, where any serious conflict of interest arises, an independent commission appointed to act jointly by the Presbytery and by the separating congregation) shall see that assets belonging to the congregation are fairly and justly dealt with, having first regard to the Overriding Objective and then all relevant circumstances, including in particular the following factors:

(i)   the nature and terms of the trusts (implied or explicit) to which the assets are or may be subject, giving due attention to the *cy pres* doctrine (see sections 6.5.1 and 6.5.4);

(ii) the views and desires of any Members of the separating congregation who wish to remain as Members of IPC and the likelihood of a continuing IPC congregation being viable;

(iii) the views and desires of any Members of the separating congregation who do not wish to remain as IPC Members;

(iv) whether any assets of the retiring congregation can properly be split between any continuing Members and any new or different organisation which departing Members are aspiring to join, and if so, in what proportions;

(v) in the event that a continuing IPC congregation is unlikely to be viable, whether the assets can properly be given in its entirety to any new or different organisation or organisations which departing members are aspiring to join, and in what proportions if more than one. [see also section 6.5].

The Presbytery liaison officer and the representative of the separating congregation shall thereby agree an appropriate disbursement of assets and timetable thereof. The separating congregation's Elders shall require to transfer out of the IPC or otherwise have ceased to be IPC Elders, at which point the congregation shall be deemed to have left the IPC and ceased to be under its care.

SECTION 10

PUBLIC WORSHIP

10.1 The Nature of Public Worship

The purpose of all creation is to serve, praise, adore, and bow down before God the Holy Trinity as its Creator, Sustainer, Lord and Master. All human beings live under the obligation to do these things, summarised by the English word 'worship', with all the faculties with which God has endowed them as God's image bearers. The Fall of our first parents is rightly seen as a refusal to worship the one true God, and that remains the heart of what sin is to the present day. The gospel, in contrast, is rightly seen as a call to true worship and a restoration to a position of true worship (in spirit and in truth, John 4:23), through the perfect worship and sacrifice and ongoing heavenly ministry of the Lord Jesus Christ.

While Christians are called to present their bodies as living sacrifices as their 'spiritual' worship, that is, to see their whole lives as worship (Romans 12:2), the primary form of worship of God's covenant people is when they assemble specifically for that purpose on the Lord's Day.

God has appointed since the creation of the world one day in seven to be kept as a Sabbath, holy to him. Since the resurrection of the Lord Jesus this has been the first day of the week. On this day the people of God are to set aside normal work, to devote the day to God, to rest, to acts of mercy, and to fellowship with his family, the Church. On this day also the Church is to gather for public worship in covenant assembly.

Before all else, an assembly for public worship is a meeting of the triune God with his covenant people. Like the first great assembly at Sinai, it is initiated by God out of his grace, and the Church's part in it is always one of response to his action in making himself known to us and calling us to know him. Services of worship are also rightly understood to have a purpose of encouraging one another (Heb 10:24–25) and proclaiming the gospel to the watching world (1 Cor 14:24–25); however, these purposes are subordinate to, and dependent upon, the primary purpose of worship, which is fellowship between God and his people.

Since worship is at God's initiative, not ours, what worship consists of is not left to the judgment of individual believers, congregations or denominations, but is laid down for us in the Word of God. In the covenant assembly God restates and confirms his covenant with his people. It is here that God brings to greatest expression the fellowship between him and his people that was promised to Abraham and realised in Christ (Gen 17:7; Exod 6:7; 1 John 1:3). God applies the blessings of the gospel to his people through the means of grace, principally prayer, the reading and preaching of the Word and the celebration of the sacraments. These are the main means through which the Holy Spirit brings about the people's fellowship with God and their transformation into the likeness of Christ.

In public worship God calls the people again to worship him; hears their confession of sins, assuring them of his forgiveness through the name of Christ; hears the people sing his praises in psalms, hymns and spiritual songs, confessing their faith in individual testimony or corporate recitation of creeds, confessions and catechisms, and presenting their requests to him in prayer; addresses the people through his Word read and preached; receives offerings from them; works in them through the sacraments of Baptism and the Lord's Supper; and sends them out with his blessing. These are the elements of worship taught in Scripture and worship should be conducted in such a way as to make them clear. While there is freedom in the form they are to take, the Church is not to add to them. This is because public worship is an obligation God lays on all people and therefore to add other elements to public worship would be to require people to worship God in ways God himself has not called them to do. Therefore rites or ceremonies not found in Scripture are not to be included.

Prayer, the reading and preaching of the Word of God and the administration of the sacraments are necessary parts of worship. None alone is sufficient, but all require the others. The absence of any is always insufficient and damaging to the Church. Furthermore, correct understanding, celebration and thanksgiving are combined together in right worship. Worship in Spirit and truth should involve the whole person, body and soul. In this way, the Church is protected from error and the believer from sinful idolatry.

A right understanding of worship is essential for a right understanding of how the church relates to its surrounding culture. First, because God calls people to worship him from every tribe and tongue and nation, it is right that the church conducts worship in the language of the people of the time and place in which it is located, endeavours to be clear and comprehensible to those people, and avoids the requirement of cultural forms, idioms, practices and dress which originate not in the Word of God but in the non-Christian culture of another time or place. Christian worship consists of the same elements, but will be expressed differently depending upon the culture and context of a particular church.

But second, because worship is initiated by God, not us, and calls us to abandon our sinful practices and replace them with worship in the manner God has commanded (both in our whole lives and in the public worship of the Church), the nature of Christian worship is not dependent upon the culture with which the church is surrounded and out of which its people have been called. Christian worship consists of the same elements, and will be substantially the same, wherever in the world and in history Christians find themselves, because it originates in the one God who does not change, is offered in his one incarnate, crucified, risen and reigning Son, and is the work of the one unchanging Spirit (Eph 4:4–6).

10.2 The Leadership of Public Worship

Christ rules over his Church by his Word and his Spirit; and so the worship leader at every Christian worship service is the Lord Jesus Christ himself. Christ applies himself and his benefits to his people by the Spirit working through prayer, the reading, preaching and teaching of the Word, sealed by the sacraments, and received in faith by prayer. He does this through the working of the Holy Spirit in his people, including the ministry of the officers of his Church.

For this reason:

(i)   The Session is responsible for the immediate oversight of the public worship of the church, and is not to delegate this responsibility to others outside the Session.

(ii)   Public worship is normally to be conducted by one or more Elders of the church, or those deemed appropriate by the Session.

(iii)   Other members of the church may give readings of Scripture, lead in prayer, or lead congregational singing, provided that they are appropriately trained and overseen by one or more of the Elders.

(iv)   The Session may allow men who are ordained as Elders in other churches or denominations to lead worship and/or to preach, provided they are satisfied as to their orthodoxy of faith and life. They may also allow other men who are deemed competent to be permitted to preach or lead worship, under the authority of the Session. At all times the Session remains responsible for all that is said in the pulpit and is to guard the pulpit with great diligence.

(v)   For the avoidance of doubt, women are not permitted to preach. This is:
a) in accordance with Christ's own practice in his appointment of apostles;
b) in obedience to the Apostles' instructions;
c) appropriate for the Church as Christ's bride, as she listens to the instruction of her Husband and Lord;
d) in accordance with the created nature of male and female in the beginning;
e) in accordance with the universal practice of the Church from the time of Christ onwards; and,

f) so as not to undermine the men, women and children of the Church in their endeavour to live and shape their lives according to the God-given roles of men and women in the Church and in the family.

It should be noted that in the kingdom of God, because of our justification only by the merits of Christ, that the role an individual plays in the Church has no relevance to that individual's importance to the Church and value in the sight of God. Therefore the limitation of the role of Elder and preacher in the Church to men neither exalts men nor denigrates women but works for the good of all the men, women and children of the Church.

(vi)   Only Elders may administer the sacraments.

10.3 Ministry of the word

Since worship is God's initiative, and our part is always response, the service should open with a call from God to the people, in the words of Scripture, to worship him.

The public reading of Scripture is an essential element of public worship. It should be read clearly and with understanding, with the aim of helping the congregation to understand themselves what is being read.

The use of Psalms and other parts of Scripture, spoken or sung together by the congregation, is encouraged.

The use of Scripture in all the elements of worship is to be encouraged. When non-scriptural hymns, songs or prayers are used, the Session must ensure that their content is in conformity to the teachings of Scripture.

The corporate recitation of the Ecumenical Creeds and Reformed Confessions and Catechisms is of great benefit to the Church, as the Church declares the faith revealed once for all in Scripture to be her own, and in doing so identifies herself with the one, holy, catholic and apostolic Church through the ages.

Central to every service is the proclamation of the Word of God in the sermon. The sermon must be a serious exposition of Scripture, which endeavours to make plain the meaning of a portion (or on occasion a theme or teaching) of Scripture as originally given, demonstrates the part it plays in the full revelation of God's purposes, and applies it to hearers today. Sermons should most commonly be expositions of a passage of Scripture which has been read in the service. These may be organised in a continuous fashion so that one week's passage follows on from where the previous week's ended; also doctrinal sermons or series of sermons are appropriate, as judged by the Session, which draw on Scripture more widely for their content. In all cases, the way in which the content of the sermon is based on the text of Scripture must be made clear, so that the people understand that what they are hearing is the Word of God not the word of men.

The preacher must endeavour to set forth the Word of God, as contained in the passage being expounded, rather than his own personal opinions. Since all Scripture is the Word of God and also the word of man, the Holy Spirit's purpose in writing it is found in looking for the human author's purpose. Therefore sermons must explain the meaning of the passage in its original context and thus what the Holy Spirit is saying to the church today. Yet sermons are not mere explanations of Scripture but also proclamation (of the coming judgment and the good news of salvation in Christ) and exhortation (to repentance from sin and faith in Christ), in the specific aspects indicated by the passage being expounded. Preachers should endeavour to be clear in explanation, direct in proclamation, and urgent and specific in application for the salvation and edification of the hearers. They should attempt to address all the different spiritual conditions which will be found in every congregation, including unbelievers who may be present, those with a poor understanding of the gospel, and among members and other professing believers, both regenerate and unregenerate. Above all, sermons must exalt Christ and call people to repentance and faith.

The service should end with God's blessing pronounced upon his covenant people, in the words of Scripture.

10.4 Sacraments

The sacraments are signs and seals of the covenant of grace, commanded by Christ as markers of the visible Church and means of grace to his elect people. They speak powerfully of our union with the crucified and risen Lord Jesus. They speak therefore of all the benefits of the gospel and confirm the participation of Christ's elect in them; they visibly mark out those who belong to Christ and not to the world; they bind them to their Lord in covenant faith and loyalty. As such they are essential elements of Christian worship.

The sacraments are not mechanical; they do not confer benefits automatically on those who participate in them. Unbelievers who participate derive no benefit from them but rather increase their condemnation. Nor, however, are the sacraments merely symbolic. When received in faith the Holy Spirit uses them to confer, mysteriously, the blessings that they symbolise.

The sacraments serve to illuminate and apply the Word of God to believers, and they require the explanation of the Word of God in order to fulfil their function. Word and sacrament are therefore not to be separated. Furthermore, it is essential that the Church exercise discipline in who is permitted to participate in the sacraments, to preserve their reinforcement of assurance for believers and to prevent the giving of false assurance to unbelievers. The power of the keys of the kingdom is exercised by granting access to or exclusion from the sacraments. For both these reasons, the sacraments are only to be administered by ordained Elders of the church, and ordinarily only in a public worship service of the church. Both Teaching and Ruling Elders (where permitted by their Presbytery) may administer them; Teaching Elders are under an obligation to do so regularly.

10.4.1 Baptism

Baptism is the sacrament given by our Lord as the sign and seal of entry into the covenant of grace, and therefore into the Church, the Body of Christ. It is commanded by Christ and his Apostles as an integral and indispensable part of becoming a Christian. Its central signification is of being united to Christ; it does this by signifying union with him in his death and resurrection, washing clean from the uncleanness of sin, and the outpouring of the Holy Spirit. While it has no saving efficacy in itself, it seals to those who receive it in faith the benefits of the things that it signifies.

Baptism is not a sign of our response to God in faith but of God's gracious initiative in making us his. It is not a sign of election, for that is invisible to us in this age. It is a sign of covenant membership, of the promises of God in Christ to those who believe. It confers covenantal responsibilities on those who receive it. Therefore baptism should not be submitted to lightly, but nor should it be delayed unduly for those professing faith in Christ and living in accordance with their confession, or born or adopted into families with such parents.

Baptism, signifying as it does the once-for-all nature of salvation through union with Christ, can not and must not be repeated. This remains true even when someone has been baptised in the past when they should not have been. Therefore a man or woman who comes to faith as an adult who has been previously baptised (for example, as an unbelieving teenager, or as an infant child of unbelieving parents) is not to be rebaptised. Rather, they should be encouraged to find out all they can about their own baptism, and consciously own and accept before the Lord the promises made by them or on their behalf on that day. In the case when a baptism was made in a non-trinitarian church, or not using the name of the Trinity, or not using water, it is to be judged that this was not a baptism at all and it is appropriate that the person should be baptised now.

Baptism is a public ceremony for the benefit not only of the person being baptised, but for the whole Church (who must constantly remember their own baptisms) and the watching world. It is not to be separated from the reading and preaching of God's Word. Therefore baptism should normally take place as part of the main service of worship on the

Lord's Day. The congregation should be notified in advance and encouraged to attend.

In the liturgies that follow for Baptism, the forms of words given for the Elder to use are suggestions which may be varied as the Session shall see fit, provided that the content is maintained (see also Appendix V). The exception to this is the baptismal formula itself which must be followed exactly. Similarly, the candidate's responses to the questions proposed may be varied as appropriate, but the words of the Apostles' Creed must be followed exactly, if used in the service.

(i) Baptism of Adults

The candidate should have been prayerfully examined by an Elder beforehand with regard to his or her understanding of baptism and therefore of the gospel. Moreover, the Elder should take care to ensure that the candidate is making a credible profession of faith and living a life consistent with that profession.

It is often appropriate to interview the candidate or ask them to give a testimony of how they have come to repent and believe in the Lord Jesus Christ.

The presiding Elder shall give an explanation of Baptism, such as this:

Baptism is a sign, commanded by Jesus, that the world is divided into two groups: those who belong to him, and those who do not; those who are part of the family of God, the Christian Church; and those who are not. When a person joins the Church of Jesus Christ that fact is marked by baptism.

Baptism is a sign of three totally undeserved, gracious things that Jesus does for Christians. First, it is a sign of being washed clean, because Christians have been washed clean from their sins by Jesus' death on the cross. Second, it is a sign of dying and rising to new life, because a Christian's old self has died and they have risen to a new life with Jesus, and there will be a day when their bodies also will be raised from the dead, as Jesus was. Third, the poured water is a sign of the Holy Spirit whom Jesus pours out on all who trust in him.

Baptism does not automatically do any of these things. But when a baptised person believes the promises contained in their baptism, God does somehow use it to do these things for them. Therefore for baptism to be of any value to the baptised person, they must love, serve and trust Jesus Christ for the rest of their life.

Statement of Faith

Elder: (name) has come to be baptised. It is therefore essential that he believes in Jesus Christ and understands his gospel. I am therefore going to ask him to affirm his own faith in the words of the Apostles' Creed.

I believe in God, the Father Almighty,
Creator of heaven and earth.
I believe in Jesus Christ, his only Son, our Lord,
who was conceived by the Holy Spirit,
born of the virgin Mary,
suffered under Pontius Pilate,
was crucified, died, and was buried;
he descended to the dead.
On the third day he rose again;

he ascended into heaven,
he is seated at the right hand of the Father,
and he will come again to judge the living and the dead.
I believe in the Holy Spirit,
the holy catholic Church,
the communion of saints,
the forgiveness of sins,
the resurrection of the body,
and the life everlasting.
Amen.

(i)   Do you believe that the death which baptism symbolises should by rights have been yours, were it not for Christ's death for you, taking the penalty for your sins?

I do.

(ii)   Do you believe that the washing from sin, new life, and outpouring of the Spirit which baptism symbolises come only through Christ's death and resurrection?

I do.

(iii)   Do you therefore understand that you can only be saved through faith in Jesus Christ, and not through anything you can do?

I do.

(iv)   Do you renounce the world, the flesh and the devil, and repent of your sins of thought, word and deed against the living God?

I do.

(v)   Do you trust in Christ alone for your salvation, and understand that you must continue to do so for your whole life, if your baptism is to be of any value to you?

I do.

Baptismal Promises

(i)   Do you therefore promise to live from this day forward in the instruction, obedience and worship of God the Father, Son and Holy Spirit?

I do.

(ii)   Do you promise, to the best of your ability and in the power of the Holy Spirit, to lead a life of devoted service to your Lord and Saviour Jesus Christ?

I do.

Congregational promise

(name) is to be baptised into the visible Church of Jesus Christ, and will become a member of this congregation. Therefore you who are members are all obliged to love and receive (him/her) as a fellow-member of Christ's body, for 'we were all baptised into one body'. Do you recognise your new responsibility to encourage him/her in his/her Christian life by godly example, prayer, exhortation and practical concern.

We do.

The Baptism

(Name) has affirmed his faith in Jesus Christ and promised to serve him with the rest of his life. I am therefore delighted to baptise him today.

[Baptism]
(Name), I baptise you in the name of the Father, the Son and the Holy Spirit.

Prayer
Our Father, we commit our brother/sister (name) to you. Please have mercy on him/her and be faithful to the promises you have made to him/her today. May he/she never know a day when he does not believe those promises and turn away from his sins and towards Jesus Christ. And may he/she be a faithful servant of Christ till the end of his/her life. In Jesus' name, Amen.

It is usual for a certificate of baptism to be provided by the Session.

(ii) Baptism of Infants

The infant children of one or both Christian parents, being born into the covenant family of the church, are to be baptised as a sign of their membership of the visible Church of Christ, in which they will grow being taught the truths of the gospel and godly habits of prayer, Bible reading and Christ-like living. This being so, only the children of church Members in good standing are normally to be baptised. Baptising the children of Non-Members would only happen in exceptional circumstances. The infant children of those who are not believers should not be baptised, as this would be inconsistent with the meaning of the sacrament. In accordance with 1 Corinthians 7:14, a child with only one believing parent may also be baptised at the discretion of the session. In this case 'parents' below should be read as referring to the one believing parent.

Baptism of whole families, upon the conversion of the parents, is to be encouraged as is exemplified for us in Acts 16:15, 33.

The parents should have been prayerfully examined by an Elder beforehand with regard to their understanding of baptism and therefore of the gospel. Moreover, the Elder should take care to ensure that the parents are making a credible profession of faith and living a life consistent with that profession.

It is often appropriate to interview the parents or ask them to give a testimony of how they have come to repent and believe in the Lord Jesus Christ.

The presiding Elder shall give an explanation of Baptism, such as this:

Model Explanation of Baptism

The Christian gospel is that God has made his Son, Jesus Christ, Lord of all. The Christian Church is those people Jesus has brought into his kingdom, who have been forgiven for their sins and now live with Jesus as their Lord. They are the family of God, who through faith in Jesus, and by the power of the Holy Spirit, know God as their Father. They are the people of God, with whom he made a covenant in the time of Abraham, that they would be his and know him as their God.

God alone knows those whom he has chosen to have genuine faith. Nevertheless, he has given signs to show visibly who is a member of Jesus' Church, and to convince them that all of God's promises and mercies in Christ apply to them, if they receive them in faith. These signs are Baptism and the Lord's Supper.

Baptism is therefore the sign that someone has joined the Christian Church. It is a sign of being washed clean, because Christians have been washed clean from their sins by Jesus' death on the cross. It is also a sign of dying and rising, because a Christian's old self has died and they have risen to a new life with Jesus. Finally, the poured water is a sign of the Holy Spirit whom Jesus pours out on all who trust in him.

Baptism does not automatically do any of these things. But when a baptised person believes the promises contained in their baptism, God uses it mysteriously to do these things for them.

As the covenant family of God, children born to members of Jesus' Church, who will be brought up believing the Christian gospel, are counted as members of his church. That is why from the beginning of the church households have been baptised because of the parents' faith in Christ. Baptism does not guarantee a child's salvation, but marks them as being part of the church family. Like all Christians, baptised children are responsible for trusting in Christ and believing his promises throughout the rest of their lives. And they are to be brought up knowing they have been baptised, counting themselves as privileged members of Jesus' Church, knowing

God as their Father and Jesus as their Saviour and Lord, and aware of their lifelong duty to serve him.

[Note: * indicates 'her' or 'she' is to be substituted when appropriate]

<u>Statement of Faith</u>

(Father and/or Mother's names) have brought (Child's name) to be baptised. It is therefore essential that they believe in Christ and will bring (name) up to do so too. I am therefore going to ask them to affirm their own faith in the words of the Apostles' Creed.

(Parent/s)
I believe in God, the Father Almighty,
Creator of heaven and earth.
I believe in Jesus Christ, his only Son, our Lord,
who was conceived by the Holy Spirit,
born of the Virgin Mary,
suffered under Pontius Pilate,
was crucified, died, and was buried;
he descended to the dead.
On the third day he rose again;
he ascended into heaven,
he is seated at the right hand of the Father,
and he will come again to judge the living and the dead.
I believe in the Holy Spirit,
the holy catholic Church,
the communion of saints,
the forgiveness of sins,
the resurrection of the body,
and the life everlasting.
Amen.

(i)   Do you believe that the death which baptism symbolises should by rights have been yours and (*child's name*)'s, were it not for Christ's death for you, taking the penalty for your sins?

I/We do.

(ii)   Do you believe that the washing from sin, new life, and outpouring of the Spirit which baptism symbolises come only through Christ's death and resurrection?

I/We do.

(iii)   Do you therefore understand that people can only be saved through faith in Jesus Christ, and not through anything they can do?

I/We do.

(iv)   Do you renounce the world, the flesh and the devil, and repent of your sins of thought, word and deed against the living God?

I/We do.

(v)   Do you trust in Christ alone for your salvation, and understand that (name) must do so too, if his* baptism is to be of any value to him*?

We do.

Baptismal Promises

(i)   Do you therefore promise to bring (name) up in the instruction, obedience and worship of the Lord, to pray for him* and with him*, to include him* in the fellowship of the church, and to be an example to him* of faith and life?

We do.

(ii)   Will you teach him* what his baptism means for him*, urge him* to repent and believe continually in the Lord Jesus Christ, and assist him* in every possible way to lead a life of devoted service to his* Lord and Saviour?

We will.

Congregational promise

(Name) is to be baptised into the visible Church of Jesus Christ, and will become a member of this congregation. Therefore we who are members are all obliged to love and receive him* as a fellow-member of Christ's body, for 'we were all baptised into one body'. Do you promise to encourage him* in his* Christian life by godly example, prayer, exhortation and practical concern?

We do.

The Baptism

(Name) has been born into the family of the church and will be brought up to know and love Jesus Christ. I am therefore delighted to baptise him today.

[Baptism]

(Name), I baptise you in the name of the Father, the Son and the Holy Spirit.

Prayer

Our Father, we commit our brother/sister (name) to you. Please have mercy on him* and be faithful to the promises you have made to him* today. As he* grows up may he* never know a day when he* does not believe those promises and turn away from his* sins and towards Jesus Christ. And may he* be a faithful servant of Christ till the end of his* life. In Jesus' name, Amen.

It is usual for a certificate of baptism to be provided by the Session.

10.4.2 Lord's Supper

The Lord's Supper is the sacrament commanded by Christ as the sign and seal of the ongoing communion between him and his people. It signifies Christ's giving of himself from heaven in union with believers; the total dependence of Christians for eternal life on Christ's giving of himself in his death; the need for ongoing reception of Christ and his benefits by repentance and faith; and the unity of the Spirit that exists between all believers in the Church. In it, to those who receive it in faith in Christ, the Holy Spirit seals all the benefits of the gospel. Those who receive the sacrament unworthily do not receive that which is signified but are guilty of the body and blood of Jesus.

(i) Frequency of Celebration

The Lord's Supper is to be celebrated frequently. The Session is to determine how frequently. Quarterly would be an absolute minimum; weekly would be entirely appropriate.

(ii) Admission to the Lord's Table

The Session shall admit to the Lord's Table those who have received Christian baptism, who in their opinion have given a credible profession of faith and who are not under discipline in another church. Those who do not profess faith in Christ, who are persisting in unrepentant sin, or who are out of fellowship with fellow-believers should not be admitted. The presiding Elder should warn such people away from the table lest they eat and drink judgment upon themselves. At the same time, he should encourage the repentant and believing sinners of the congregation to partake, reminding them that the Supper is a means of grace for them.

It is proper for those being admitted for the first time, including covenant children, to be examined by the Session as to their faith in Christ, their understanding of the gospel and the sacrament, and their ability to examine themselves in accordance with 1 Corinthians 11:28. There is no minimum age for this, but in the case of covenant children both the parents and the Session must be satisfied that they meet these criteria, the Session having the final decision.

If a believer comes to the Session who is under discipline from another church, that person may be admitted if the Session is convinced that there has been true repentance for sins committed and proper attempts at rectifying the situation have been made.

(iii) Administration of the Lord's Supper

The Lord's Supper should be administered as part of a worship service that includes the preaching of the Word. It is fitting that the Supper follow on from the preaching of the Word so the people move from being instructed by the Lord to communion with him.

The Elder should read the words of institution of the Lord's Supper as found in 1 Corinthians 11 or one of the Gospels. In addition, he may read other words of instruction, such as from 1 Corinthians 10 or John 6.

The Elder shall explain the meaning of the Lord's Supper, showing the connection where appropriate to the content of the sermon just preached.

Model explanation of the Lord's Supper

The Lord Jesus instituted the Lord's Supper for his Church as a perpetual memorial of his death for her until his return. It is not a sacrifice but a remembrance of his once-for-all sacrifice of himself for the sins of his people. It is not only a memorial, but a means by which God feeds us with the crucified, risen and exalted Christ. In it God promises to his people that if they receive him with faith, Christ is made one with them by the work of the Holy Spirit. As we receive the bread and the wine, we receive by faith Christ and all the benefits of his suffering and death. In this Supper, then, God calls us to deeper gratitude for our salvation, greater repentance of our sin, and renewed commitment to obey him, as we wait for the great wedding feast of the Lamb when he returns, of which this meal is a foretaste and a pledge.

The Lord's Supper is also a pledge of the communion which believers have with Christ and with each other. As Scripture says, 'we who are many are one body, for we all partake of the one bread.' As we come to the Lord's Table, we are humbly to resolve to deny ourselves, put to death our sinful nature, resist the temptation of the devil, and commit ourselves again to the service of Christ and his people who bear his name.

The Elder shall declare Christ's invitation to his Table to all who are baptised believers, living penitent lives, and members in good standing (or equivalent) of Christian churches. He shall exhort them to receive from Christ as they eat and drink all that is signified by the Supper.

He shall warn the unbaptised, the unbelieving, the impenitent, and those out of fellowship with other believers against participation, for fear of eating and drinking judgment on themselves. At the same time, he should make clear that the Lord calls them to repentance and faith and promises them all the benefits of the gospel, signified by the Lord's Supper, should they do so.

The Elder shall offer prayer for the Holy Spirit to work in Christ's people as they receive the Supper, and thanksgiving for the elements and all that they signify.

The Elder shall break the bread in the sight of the people and say the following or similar words:

Our Lord Jesus, on the night when he was betrayed, took the bread and having blessed it, broke it and gave it to his disciples saying: Take, eat; this is my body which is given for you. Do this in remembrance of me.'

He shall take the cup in the sight of the people, and say the following or similar words:

After they had eaten the bread, our Lord Jesus took the cup and gave it to his disciples saying: 'This is my blood of the new covenant, which is shed for you.'

A prayer of thanksgiving shall be offered by the Elder.

Congregational prayer, such as the Lord's Prayer, or singing, is an appropriate response.

SECTION 11

DISCIPLINE

11.1 Procedures for Discipline

Discipline is the exercise of the authority which the Lord Jesus has given to the Church. It is for the purity and peace of the Church and the honour of the Lord Jesus Christ. Its purpose is to bring about reconciliation of man to God and man to man.

Ecclesiastical discipline is primarily pastoral, not magisterial; that is, its power is moral or spiritual and it acts without resort to legal force. Furthermore, all Church power is solely ministerial and declarative, for the Holy Scriptures are the only infallible rule of faith and practice. This does not mean that the Church courts will refrain from reporting suspected criminal activity to the police or, in the case of a child at risk of harm from the suspected behaviour of a Member, to the appropriate state authorities; on the contrary, the Church court involved, in appropriate cases, will do so without delay.

All offences, being sins against God, are grounds for discipline. This includes those which are private or known to few people, those which are public, and those which may not cause harm to others.

The local church Session also has original jurisdiction over its Members including Deacons as officers in that local church. Presbytery has original jurisdiction over its Elders. Original jurisdiction over a judiciary belongs to the next broader judiciary.

In cases where the judiciary which has original jurisdiction is unable or unwilling to exercise necessary discipline, the next broader court may do so, but only if sufficient cause for this has been demonstrated.

A charge may be brought by a judiciary or any Member of an IPC church who has knowledge of the situation. A complaint by a Non-Member must be brought to a judiciary for their consideration. Any individual person who brings charges shall be warned that if reasonable grounds for the charges have not been demonstrated, the accuser himself may be censured for slander. The Church court will not consider any charges based on rumours or hearsay, but may investigate where a specific offence is widely believed to have taken place and raises the strong possibility of the guilt of the accused. The Church court should dismiss any charges in cases where the charge, even if proven true, is not serious enough to warrant trial.

Charges serious enough to warrant trial can be in areas of conduct and practice or in areas of doctrine. A charge should be brought for offences which disturb the peace, purity, or unity of the Church.

In areas of doctrine, for a non-ordained church Member, the offence must be one which constitutes a denial of the faith. For an ordained officer in the church, an offence in areas of doctrine serious enough to warrant trial is in cases where there is a violation of his ordination vows or the doctrinal standards as expressed in the confessional statements of the IPC (the Westminster Standards and the Three Forms of Unity).

Any charge which would require a sanction stronger than a rebuke shall not be progressed without a trial.

Every charge brought before a Church court must be brought in writing. It must provide sufficient detail as to the facts of the offence, including, as much as is possible, the time and circumstances of the offence. It must give applicable references to the Word of God, and where applicable, to the confessional standards of the IPC. It shall provide the names of the witnesses of the offence and give details as to any other type of evidence. The Moderator or Clerk who receives the charge shall specify the date it was received.

Where the charge has not been brought in written form and where the charge, if proved true, would constitute an offence serious enough to warrant trial, the Church court should not dismiss it on the basis of any technicality. It shall require that the charge and the specifications of the details be put in the proper form and, where applicable, help the accuser put the charges in the proper form.

A charge shall not allege more than one offence. Several charges against the same person may be brought at the same time and tried together. Each charge must be accompanied with the proper specifications. A vote on each charge shall be taken separately.

No charge shall be admitted if it is filed more than two years after the alleged offence has taken place unless there are exceptional circumstances.

If the offender confesses, the way is clear for the court either to restore him or to impose such censure as the welfare of the offender and/or the church may require.

11.2 Personal Offences

If a personal offence has been committed, public or private, the person offended should seek to follow the steps prescribed by our Lord in bringing about reconciliation (Matt 18:15–17). If the offence is minor, he should overlook the offence as 'love covers over a multitude of sins' (1 Pet 4:8; Prov 10:12). If the offence is more serious, he shall, in Christian love, go to the person and seek to bring about reconciliation. If attempts at reconciliation have failed, the matter may be brought to the Church court which has jurisdiction. The Church court shall make sure that the injured party has sought appropriately to implement the steps our Lord prescribed in Matthew 18. In normal cases, private offences should only be admitted if the course set out in Matthew 18 has been followed. Even in the case of public offences, it may be appropriate for the Church court to seek reconciliation in terms of Matthew 18.

A charge against an Elder should normally be admitted only if it is brought by two or more witnesses (1 Tim 5:19).

11.3 Session

It is the duty of the Session to protect the purity of the local church and the honour of the Lord Jesus Christ. The jurisdiction of the Session is over those whose names are on the rolls of the church, both communicant and non-communicant Members.

One of the duties of the Session, in the course of their pastoral care and oversight of Members of the congregation, is to exercise careful and loving discipline with the overall object being the restoration and reconciliation of a Member who is being persistently and seriously disobedient to the Lord Jesus Christ.

11.4 Appeal to Broader Church Courts

One or more Members of a church who have concerns about one or more Elders' teaching, doctrine or life should raise them with the individual(s) concerned or where necessary discuss them with the Session. Where other problems of disagreement or conflict involving one or more Elders (including the Session) arise, members should raise them with the individual(s) concerned or where necessary discuss them with the Session. If resolution is not possible, or such discussion is not appropriate, they may appeal to Presbytery.

Appeals to Presbytery should be made in writing to the Presbytery Clerk or Moderator. Presbytery has discretion over whether to admit an appeal for consideration or not.

Any Member involved in a dispute or Elder (including the Session) who considers the decision of the Presbytery is erroneous having regard to the Overriding Objective may appeal to Synod. Appeals to Synod should be made in writing to the Synod Clerk or Moderator. Synod has discretion over whether to admit an appeal for consideration or not.

11.5 Trial Procedure

Before trial, the Church court involved must decide whether the case warrants consideration. If the Church court deems that the case is not serious enough to warrant consideration or if for any other reason it decides that it will not hear the case, this will be communicated in writing to the accuser. The Church court involved may decide to refer the case for trial to a judicial commission appointed by the court.

Judicial cases should be heard as quickly as possible. Prosecution of the offence must begin within one year of when the charge has been made.

When in a judicial capacity, Church courts shall normally be in open Session. This shall always be the case when a charge of false doctrine is brought. In other cases, where the needs of discipline or the delicacy of the charge warrants it, the trial can proceed in closed session upon a vote of at least two thirds of the court's Members.

At the beginning of every trial and at every subsequent meeting of the trial judiciary, the Moderator shall announce: 'This body is about to sit in a judicial capacity. I exhort you, the members, to bear in mind your solemn duty to faithfully minister and declare the Word of God and to submit all your judgments to its infallible rule.'

In unusual circumstances the court may deny the accused the right of participating in the Lord's Supper or the performing of the functions of his office until the case is concluded.

Citations must be written and should ordinarily be served in person. Where that is not possible, they should be sent by certified mail.

If the accused fails to appear before the Session without satisfactory reason for his absence given before the time of the case, he will be summoned a second time. If he still does not appear, the trial will proceed in his absence.

In a trial before a Presbytery, if the accused fails to appear without satisfactory reason given before the time of his case, the trial will proceed in his absence. When an accused person fails to appear before a court, he shall be suspended from the sacraments and/or any office in the church pending decision of the court. In the event the accused fails to appear before a court of the Church, a counsel will be appointed to represent the accused. The relevant court may impose whatever censure it finds warranted.

The accused may request a change in the time of meeting due to an inability to be present or because of a need for additional time to prepare his defence.

At the first meeting of the trial when the court begins consideration of the alleged offence, the charge and the specifications shall be read. At this first meeting, except by consent of both parties, the only actions which will be taken are:

(i)   The charges and specifications will be read and formally presented to the accused. These will include the names of any witnesses and copies of any documents which may be presented against him.

(ii)   The time, date, and place of the next meeting of the trial will be decided and communicated in written form to both parties. It shall not be less than two weeks from the first meeting.

(iii)   The accused shall be granted the possibility of calling witnesses. All parties and their witnesses shall be cited to appear and heard at the next meeting of the trial.

The court shall appoint a clerk who will detail the charges made, a list of the members present at each session, and he will keep an accurate record of the trial. The following must be included:

(i)   the charge and the specifications;

(ii)   any objections made and exceptions taken;

(iii)   a list of witnesses and a summary of their testimony;

(iv)   all rulings and decisions of the judiciary;

(v)   the minutes of any private deliberations. These minutes, together with all relevant papers, shall be certified by the trial judiciary and submitted to the next broader court in cases of appeal.

Where deemed appropriate, the court may appoint a prosecutor. He must be a Member in good standing of the IPC. Normally, he should also be a member of the court that is conducting the trial.

11.6 The Accused

The accused is entitled to the assistance of a counsel who may represent the accused before the court. The counsel must be a member in good standing in the IPC. If the accused does not identify a counsel the judiciary, if it deems appropriate, may appoint a counsel for him.

The accused may not sit in judgment on his own case in at any stage. No person who is counsel in a judicial case may sit in judgment on the same case once he has been appointed counsel.

The accused may take exception to any and all rulings or decisions made by the judiciary and register an appeal with the next broader court (as below).

The accused shall be allowed one copy of the minutes at the expense of the judiciary. Additional copies of the minutes may be obtained by him at cost.

11.7 Witnesses and Evidence

Every court shall be its own judge as to who shall be admitted as witnesses in a case. Either party has the right to challenge witnesses that may be called to testify. The accused may object to the admissibility or relevance of any evidence produced to support the charge. He shall give reasons for his challenge and the court shall decide if the witnesses or evidence will be used.

Private writings, printed publications, and statements in electronic media such as blog posts shall be received as evidence of the author's opinion where genuineness and authorship can be clearly established.

The accused may be allowed to testify, but shall not be compelled to do so. No inference of guilt may be drawn from his failure to testify.

When the charge depends entirely on the testimony of witnesses, at least two credible witnesses shall be necessary to establish the charge. But when there is sufficient corroborating evidence, the testimony of one witness may be considered sufficient to establish a charge.

Husbands and wives, parents and children, shall not be required to testify against each other.

Before giving testimony, every witness shall be solemnly admonished that his testimony is given as before the Lord and that he/she is to tell the truth, the whole truth, and nothing but the truth on the matters on which he/she is called to testify.

No witness shall present testimony in the presence of other witnesses except where the witness who hears the testimony is a member of the judiciary. All testimony given shall be given in the presence of the accused except where the accused, after citation, has failed to present himself before the court.

Where unusual circumstances require it, the judiciary may direct the taking of testimony by a commission that it appoints. The commission may be another Church court of the IPC other than the one trying the case.

The court shall appoint one of its members to examine the witnesses. Other members of the court have the right to take part in the examination. Where the witnesses are produced in support of the charge, they shall first be examined by the court. The accused or his counsel may then cross-examine the witnesses. If the judiciary then asks further questions, the accused shall be given the opportunity to cross-examine. Witnesses summoned in support of the accused shall first be examined by the accused and then cross-examined by the judiciary.

New evidence discovered during the trial may be admitted, but where the evidence sustains the charge, the accused shall be given reasonable time to investigate it and supplement his defence.

11.8 Second Meeting of the Trial

At the second meeting of the trial, the accused may file any objections concerning the regularity of the proceedings up to that point, the jurisdiction of the court, the right of any member to participate in the trial, the form of the charge, the relevance or admissibility of the evidence, the competency of the witnesses, or any other substantial objections which affect the regularity of the proceedings. The accused must enter a plea of 'guilty' or 'not guilty' and this will be entered on his record. If the plea is 'guilty', the trial judiciary shall decide his censure. If the plea is 'not guilty' or if he declines to answer, a plea of 'not guilty' shall be entered on the record and the trial shall proceed. The proceedings may extend over as many meetings as are necessary for their completion.

Absence from the second or any subsequent meetings of the trial shall disqualify a member from voting thereafter and the computation of a quorum. It will not disqualify him from any other right as a member of the trial judiciary. If there is not a quorum, the trial shall be postponed to a later time.

When all the evidence against the accused has been presented and he has had the opportunity to cross-examine the witnesses, the accused shall have the right to move for the dismissal of the charges. If the motion is denied by the judiciary, the accused may then present evidence in his defence.

After all the evidence is presented, the accused may make his final argument with respect to the evidence and the law of the Church. The trial judiciary, after careful consideration, shall vote on each charge separately.

In order for a guilty verdict to be pronounced on any charge or specification, the evidence must be such as to put the conclusion beyond reasonable doubt. If the trial judiciary decides that the accused is guilty, it shall proceed to determine the censure.

The trial judiciary shall announce its decision on each charge. If the accused has been found guilty, the judiciary shall state what censure it intends to pronounce against the accused.

No person who has been found innocent shall be re-tried for that same offence. If, however, after trial, new evidence is discovered that the accused believes important, it is his right to ask a new trial and within the power of the court to grant his request.

11.9 Appeals

The accused shall have 10 days to notify the judiciary of his intention to make an appeal. If the judiciary has not been notified, the sentence shall be pronounced and the court shall proceed to apply the appropriate censure. All censures may be administered or announced in the absence of the offender, but not without due notice having been given to the offender. The making of an appeal suspends the sentence until the matter has been decided by the next broader court. However, in the case of a sentence of deposition or suspension, the sentence shall be considered in force until the matter is decided.

The accused shall have 10 days to register an appeal with the next broader court. The appeal, however, should not be refused if reasons for unavoidable delay can be demonstrated. He must provide grounds for making the appeal. Grounds for an appeal include:

(i)   irregularity in the proceedings of the more local court which have had a demonstrably negative impact on the rights of the accused;

(ii)   receiving of improper or declining to receive proper evidence;

(iii)   hurrying to a decision before proper testimony is taken;

(iv)   evidence of prejudice or bias in a case;

(v)   a mistake or an injustice in judgment or sanction.

Appeals can only be made to the next broader court unless the next broader court gives express permission otherwise. Appeals should be made in writing and lodged with the Moderator or Clerk of the next broader court.

Upon receiving notice that an appeal has been made, the Clerk of the trial judiciary shall submit the entire record of the case to the Clerk of the appellate judiciary. This shall be done within 30 days of his receiving the notice. If the next broader court does not find evidence of error or wrong doing, the ruling of the more local court shall stand.

The decision of all Church courts, with exception of the Synod, are subject to investigation and review by a broader court. A broader court may decide to review a decision even if no appeal has been made. A decision shall not be reversed unless an appeal has been made. If a review indicates irregularity of proceedings which require correction, a broader court may send the proceedings back to the trial judiciary for a new trial. If the broader court finds that there are corrections to be made, the more local court shall be required to review and correct its proceedings as soon as possible. When a judgment of a more local court is before a broader court, the appellant and the members of the trial judiciary may not propose or second motions nor vote in any decisions concerning the case.

Any matters of discipline or details unprovided for are left to the judgment of the court having jurisdiction in the case.

11.10 Application of Censures

When a court has completed the judicial process and found the person guilty, the court, unless it has received written notice of appeal within 10 days of the decision, shall proceed to apply the appropriate censure. All censures may be administered or announced in the absence of the offender, but not without due notice having been given to the offender.

Censures may relate to standing in the church, church office, or both. Censures regarding church office may or may not be accompanied by censures regarding church standing; officers censured regarding their church standing will also be censured regarding their office.

The degrees of discipline for church standing are admonition, rebuke, suspension, and excommunication.

The degrees of discipline for church office are admonition, rebuke, suspension and deposition.

a. **Admonition** is kindly and gently confronting an offender with his sin, warning him of his danger, and exhorting him to repentance. This is to be administered in private.

b. **Rebuke** is stronger and consists in a severe expression of disapproval, and an exhortation to repentance and greater obedience to the Lord Jesus Christ. When the offence is private, the rebuke shall be administered in private, but where the offence is public, the rebuke shall generally be public as well. A written statement of the offence and rebuke shall be administered as well.

c. **Suspension** is for serious offences. It consists in a temporary suspension from the privileges of membership, office, or both. This censure becomes necessary because of the seriousness of the offence or when, despite repeated admonition, an offence is persistently repeated. This may be for a definite or indefinite time.

Suspension from membership means that the person is for the specified time excluded from participation at the Lord's Table. Except in cases where the offence includes disruption of public worship or intimidation of one or more Members of the church, this does not mean exclusion from attendance at public worship.

Suspension from office means that a church officer is suspended from the duties of office for a time. This does not necessarily mean that they are suspended from the Lord's Supper, but if they are suspended from the Lord's Supper, they will also be suspended from their office. When an Elder has been suspended, the judiciary shall immediately notify all the Presbyteries of the IPC. If also suspended from the Lord's Table, he may be restored to the Lord's Table without necessarily being restored to office.

This censure should, as a rule, be announced in the church by a representative of the court. If in the judgment of the court, however, the good of the offender and/or the church requires, it may be administered privately.

d.   **Deposition** is depriving a church officer of his office. It is more severe than suspension from office. It is a solemn declaration that the offending person is no longer an officer in the church.

When an Elder, whether Ruling or Teaching, is deposed from his office, his name shall immediately be erased from the rolls of church officers. The Synod and all the Presbyteries of the IPC shall be notified of his removal and the censure of deposition will also be read publicly to the congregation by a member of Presbytery. In the case of a Teaching Elder, he shall declare the pulpit vacant. When a Deacon is deposed from his office, the censure shall be read to the congregation by a member of his Session.

A deposed officer may continue as a Member of an IPC church where he demonstrates repentance for his sin.

e.   **Excommunication** is the final censure for persistent impenitence. It is the judicial dismissal of an offender from membership in the church and therefore from fellowship at the Lord's Table. It shall be announced in the church in which the person holds membership. Its purpose, as in other types of discipline, is to bring the excommunicated person to repentance and to reconcile him once again to God.

Especially in cases of suspension, deposition, or excommunication the person censured shall be the object of earnest prayer that they may be restored.

Cases of suspension shall be reviewed by the court to determine whether the offender has shown repentance and may be restored. Cases of indefinite suspension shall be reviewed not less than 12 months after the imposition of the censure. The court shall decide if the suspension should be continued or increased to deposition or excommunication or both. No further trial is necessary to increase the censure of suspension from church office to deposition or the censure of suspension from the privileges of church membership to expulsion. This shall be recorded in the minutes. The increase in the censure is subject to appeal.

11.11 Restoration

Restoration is the result of God's grace and mercy. It is the goal of discipline.

An offender is to be restored by the same Church court which censured him or by the authority of a broader court. The act of restoration may be publicly announced or administered privately. In deciding how this is to be done, the court shall take into consideration the good of the offender and the Church.

An offender desiring restoration shall make application to the court which censured him. He shall acknowledge his offence and express his desire to be restored to the privileges of the church. This does not release the church from its responsibility in pursuing the repentance and restoration of the offender.

If the court is satisfied with the sincerity of the offender's repentance, he may be restored. There is no degree of guilt that automatically precludes the restoration of an offender to full church privileges. Being restored to the privileges of church membership does not automatically effect or imply restoration to church office. When a Member is restored, he is, as one claiming God's covenant promises offered in the gospel, to be received by the church as a brother.

An officer may be restored to his office only if the judiciary has assured itself that the restoration will not injure the witness of the Church, and that the sin of which he has now repented will not have a damaging effect on his ongoing ministry. In the case of discipline for a serious moral failure it would be exceptional for a man to be restored to office, given the biblical requirement that an overseer must be 'above reproach' and a deacon must be 'blameless' (1 Tim 3:2, 10).

11.12 Withdrawal or Dissolution of Office

Presbytery may divest an Elder without censure.

If an Elder joins another denomination without letter of transfer, his Presbytery, after assuring itself of his withdrawal, shall record his withdrawal and his standing as an Elder. When the honour of the Church requires, it shall inform the body with which the Elder has connected as to his standing.

If an Elder is no longer able to adhere to his ordination vows regarding the doctrinal standards of the Church, he should notify Presbytery of the change in his doctrinal views. Presbytery shall attempt to help resolve his difficulties. Upon failure to resolve the difficulties, Presbytery shall request his resignation, and/or depose him of his office. It shall record the event in its minutes and send a written confirmation of the deposition to the Elder, stating the reasons for the separation. His name shall be removed from the rolls of Presbytery. Depending on the circumstances, this may be a censurable offence.

In the event that a Teaching Elder fails to seek a charge, but devotes himself to other pursuits, the Presbytery shall remove the Teaching Elder's name from the rolls of Presbytery divesting him of his office.

If a Teaching Elder, Ruling Elder, or Deacon demonstrates that he lacks the gifts necessary to fulfil his duties or if he fails adequately to perform his duties, he shall be divested of his office. Also in cases where permanent physical or mental disability prevents him from exercising his office, it may be appropriate to divest the officer of his office. This does not imply that an officer who has retired or been retired because of advanced age is to be divested of his office or prevented from performing the duties related to his office. He should normally be moved to retired status.

Dissolution of the office of Teaching or Ruling Elder shall be done by his Presbytery or, where warranted, by Synod. Dissolution of the office of a Deacon shall be done by his Session.

An officer who has been divested of his office and is subsequently elected to that office shall be viewed as receiving initial election to that office.

If a congregation desires to be relieved of its Teaching Elder, it may in a duly called meeting ask him to resign by three-quarters majority vote. If the Teaching Elder agrees to do so, the Presbytery shall be requested to dissolve the relationship as of a mutually agreeable date. If the Teaching Elder is unwilling, the congregation may petition Presbytery to remove him from office and may send representatives to Presbytery to support their request. The Presbytery may grant their request, but only after giving opportunity to the Teaching Elder for his reasons for not concurring. The Presbytery may also decline the request urging the congregation to reconsider their decision. The Presbytery's decision is subject to appeal.

SECTION 12

ANNEXES

I: Explanatory Notes for the Fourth Edition of the BCO

GENERAL NOTES

This revision of the Book of Church Order (BCO) was required principally to respond to the growth of the IPC for which we are grateful to God. The review committee have made stylistic changes to unify the laws and guidance of the IPC into one document, 'The Book of Church Order (4th edn)', with the aim that this document shall be a clearly readable, useful text to support the activities of our Church.

In a denomination with Members speaking many languages across many countries, one vital aspect of this revision has been to maintain accessible and readily translatable content. Certain nation-specific references have therefore necessarily been omitted in favour of principles that can be extrapolated into the local context by a given Presbytery. For example, the need for child protection is universal but the legislative framework will differ between jurisdictions. Some language has also been clarified in the hope to avoid ambiguity or confusion in translation.

In stipulating the content of services the committee have generally followed the Regulative Principle of the Westminster Divines, that is to say, 'only that which is mandated by explicit instruction of Scripture or logically required as a good and necessary consequence of Scripture's statements [is] appropriate for the public worship of God' (p. 56, *Christ Centred Worship*, Bryan Chapell [Michigan: Baker Academic, 2009]).

Most particularly, the committee has sought to clarify the appropriate locus of powers and responsibilities in the councils (and where judicial matters are under consideration these are known as the courts) of the Church and to make explicit the distinction between law (which must be followed) and guidance (where there is scope for variance). These changes do not preclude, indeed they mandate individual Presbyteries to develop specific and suitable policy in areas where the BCO does not make a directive.

The previous BCO had been a minor revision in 2011 of the first edition having been enacted by the Synod in June 2003, following 49 years of IPC history. It followed protracted drafting work at the committee stage, when broad comparisons were made with other Presbyterian BCOs and simplicity was regarded as a prime aim. Much of it derived from the principles and practices set out in the IPC Constitution of 1978, which in turn was taken from Francis Schaeffer's older adopted version (Francis Schaeffer being the founder of IPC in 1954). The revision committee of this 4th edition has sought to align our practice with other Presbyterian codes and practices where our own was previously silent; this is perhaps most clearly exemplified in the new 'worship' and 'discipline' sections, which have drawn wisdom from the EPCEW, Free Church, OPC and PCA equivalents.

This version of the BCO incorporates constitutional elements, procedural code, practice and guidance in so far as they are necessary for the government of the Church. The revision committee have deliberately not included position statements and other supporting documentation which retain their status within those councils which have adopted them. The laying down of clear understanding and expectations in key areas of procedural code, regarded as essential for the smooth running of the Church, has been included.

In seeking to express shared understanding of IPC policy, each revision of the BCO necessarily makes changes which might impact on extant custom and practice in the local church. It is not anticipated that this BCO will impact precipitously on established local church custom and practice. There is nevertheless a real expectation that each Session will give priority to aligning their church with the BCO. Sessions must not introduce any new area of practice which deviates further from the BCO. In all things there should be a determined convergence of local practice towards that described in the BCO for the peace and harmony of our denomination. It is in this light that the BCO content should be considered.

TERMINOLOGY NOTES

This BCO refers to the Church as 'she' reflecting her status as the bride of Christ.

The upper case Church has been used in this BCO when referring to the historical and ongoing body of believers, or when referring to the whole IPC whereas the lower case church has been used when referring to individual local church groupings.

'Lords Table' has been used by convention in this BCO although 'Lords Supper' is recognised to be an equivalent term.

SPECIFIC NOTES

i. **SECTION 1**

There have been only minor changes from the previous wording.

1.4 — This BCO places the authority to amend its contents firmly in the hands of the Synod as the broadest council of the Church and its court of last appeal. The committee consider that governance of the Church can only be effected by a single agreed BCO for a given Synod.

ii. **SECTION 2**

This is a new section of the BCO. Its purpose is to explain the relationship between the councils of the Church. We consider this should be particularly helpful for a newcomer to IPC to understand our system of Church governance.

2.2 — The voting procedures for all councils of the Church are herein explained. They have been simplified so that any quorate meeting is able to make definitive decisions in all councils. It is not considered appropriate to rely on those who have not participated in the discussion to legitimise the decisions taken in a given council of the Church.

'Special business' is a defined category of decision-making, where the weight of the matter requires more than a simple majority, but the decision shall still rest with those who are present and have weighed the discussion. Advanced notice of special business is a requirement, protecting the church from precipitant change in such matters.

Formal decisions involving motions and amendments are described. They are not anticipated to be required for consensus-based decision-making but are included for the infrequent occasions where formal procedures are required, such as subsequent amendment of this BCO.

iii.   **SECTION 3**

A new section on church membership has been formed in this BCO.

9.8 — Forms of words to be used in public declarations of faith are suggested but are not intended to be prescriptive. Including an explicit acknowledgement of the oversight of the IPC is considered helpful.

iv.   **SECTION 4**
The Committee have included a separate Diaconate section to clarify the roles and responsibilities of the office of Deacon. A formal ordination process across the denomination is now included this in the BCO.

v.   **SECTION 5**

5.1 — The role of Elders is clarified here. It is recognised that within our denomination, while there is consensus that there is parity of authority, there is legitimate difference concerning the emphasis on the roles of Ruling and Teaching Elders. The description given seeks to recognise and affirm the distinctiveness and value of Ruling Elders as much as that of Teaching Elders. While it is the specific duty of Teaching Elders, it is acknowledged that Ruling Elders are able to undertake ministry of Word and sacrament in the IPC.

5.2 — The appointment process has been clarified and the order and nature of congregational involvement has been made explicit. All options for the timing of congregational involvement in the process have been considered. It was concluded that it must precede Presbytery examination, otherwise the definitive appointing role of Presbytery would become inappropriately subject to the veto of a congregation. For that reason, a congregational vote is stipulated as the initiator of formalised Elder-appointment processes. It has been emphasised that the congregation must be made aware that its vote is an initiator or a recommendation to Presbytery but does not necessarily lead to ordination as Elder in all cases.

Further detail of Presbytery-specific processes has been removed from this BCO. This is not because it does not matter, but rather because this detail belongs in policy and practice statements of a given Presbytery where there should be capacity for variation between Presbyteries.

5.6 — The accountability of Elders who are not part of a Session was given careful consideration. It is recognised that there is more than one way to achieve this but that the most effective way to ensure accountability and real relationship was considered to be allocation to an extant Session.

5.11 — The BCO has hitherto referred to other Presbyterian denominational practices in respect of discipline. It was not considered appropriate that this continue, since it essentially tied the disciplinary procedures of the IPC to the practices of another organisation. There is therefore presented in a separate 'Discipline Section' a set of procedures that closely parallel the practice of other reformed Presbyterian denominations, yet which can be wholly owned, and if required revised, by the IPC.

5.15 —Vows have been unified across the denomination in clear language.

The ordination vows of Elders are here slightly modified to recognise the different emphasis in role for Teaching and Ruling Elders. It should be noted that neither Teaching nor Ruling Elder is precluded from any function by this change — it is purposed to emphasise the very real expectation placed upon Teaching Elders to be the regular (i.e. week in week out) preachers of the Word, reflecting their principal employment in this role.

The Three Forms of Unity have been included as an equivalent subordinate standard to the Westminster Standards in this edition.

vi.   **SECTION 6**

6.2.3 — There has been a minor amendment here to remove routine voting capacity for co-opted Elders to a Session. It is not generally appropriate for an Elder to be accountable to one denomination, yet have a vote over the business of another denomination in which he has no membership and therefore no accountability.

6.5.3 — This section of Session duties brings some guidance on compliance with national (secular) law yet emphasises that God's law is supreme.

6.5.4 — Trusteeship has been retained in concept, though it is recognised that in different national jurisdictions it is likely to be manifest differently. The underlying responsibility of Elders to operate with legal authority over assets is clarified. Further, the circumstances under which local church resources should be referred to Presbytery are made clear.

It is the intent here to preserve the local church as the 'asset holder'.

vii.   **SECTION 7**

7.3 — The interrelationship between Presbytery and Synod required clarification. Autonomy of Presbytery to make policy in all areas save those where there is an impact beyond the Presbytery has been emphasised.

7.6 — References to specific national practices (i.e. guideline remuneration) have been removed deliberately. A Presbytery may of course choose to adopt such as a code of practice in its own jurisdiction.

7.9 — Just as Sessions report to Presbyteries, it is considered important that Presbyteries in turn report to the Synod.

viii.   **SECTION 8**

There was almost no content in the previous BCO to define Synod and its practices. This was one of the principal reasons for this revision of the BCO.

This revision introduces Synod procedures which in large part will sit comfortably with extant practice and largely mirrors procedures at Presbytery level, recognising the requirement for Synod to act as the broadest court and therefore the final arbiter of Church affairs.

8.5 — The Review Board is a new concept. It is considered necessary to cope with the real possibility that an appeal may be lodged with Synod many months before it may meet to hear it (potentially 11 months away if it immediately follows a Synod meeting). It would not be practicable to reconvene Synod ad hoc to deal with issues as they arise month by month. Therefore, a Review Board shall act for Synod between its sittings. The balance of presumption has been taken to uphold the decisions of Presbyteries, for it is anticipated these will not generally err. Nevertheless, the capacity for an individual to appeal to Synod is an important one in Presbyterianism and is reflected in the description of a Review Board.

8.7 — In defining matters of significant change, the Synod is empowered to call before it areas of Presbytery decision which are considered errant. As the broadest council of the Church, it must be able to act *ex novo*.

ix.   **SECTION 9**

This section contains the responsibilities of a Presbytery to operate oversight of churches within its care.

The detailed content, specifically the definition of types of churches was only recently incorporated into the BCO and has been reproduced unchanged. However, consideration as to whether this would more helpfully sit at Presbytery document level (rather than at Synod level in this BCO) may be needed in future.

x.   **SECTION 10**

A new section on 'public worship' is included to give guidance on aspects of the service and particularly on the sacraments.

10.4 — The forms of words to be used in Baptism have been somewhat simplified in this revision to make it more readily translatable. It should be noted that historically practice has varied considerably between individual churches within the IPC.

The original form of words from Francis Schaeffer's booklet and from the 3rd edition of the BCO are included in Annexe IV.

xi.   **SECTION 11**

A new section on discipline is included to guide the Church where the previous BCO relied on the processes of other denominations. It is important that the IPC own its processes, so that they can be modified if required and relied upon.

xii.   **SECTION 12**

Annexes to the BCO (except for annexe 5, where amendments have been adopted subsequently) do not form part of its substance, but may be helpful as supporting documentation.

II: Glossary

Accountability	Line of responsibility.
Appellate judiciary	The broader court of the Church that has authority to hear an appeal and review the decisions of a more local court. For example, if an appeal is made against a decision of Presbytery the appellate judiciary is the Synod.
Book of Church Order/'BCO'	The document describing the government or polity of the Church and specifying its practices and doctrines.
Broader council/court	Refers to the council/court with broader representation than the more local council/court. Synod is broader than Presbytery which is broader than Session. In contrast Session is a 'more local' council/court than Presbytery.
Caucus	A private meeting typically in the middle of another public meeting
Committee	A committee shall study and recommend action or carry out decisions already made by a council of the Church. It shall make a full report to the council that created it, and its recommendations shall require action by that body. It does not have power to act in its own

right.

Commission	E.g.: The Candidates and Credentials' Committee. A commission is empowered to consider and conclude matters referred to it by a council of the Church. The designating council shall state specifically the scope of the commission's powers and any restrictions on those powers.
Constitution	E.g.: The Review Board of Synod. The original declaration of the Constitution of the IPC was dated 11 April 1978, incorporating in the schedule and older material.
Congregational government	Government or rule primarily by the congregation as over against elected Elders.
Council	The councils of the Church range from those most local (the congregation and its Session) through Presbytery to the broadest council, the Synod.
Cy près doctrine	This is a legal concept finding expression in UK, European and North American jurisprudence. It allows, when the original objective of a Trust becomes impossible to effect, to have the terms of the Trust amended so it may continue to maintain its assets directed at the closest possible ongoing purpose of

	the Trust. In the IPC, this would be to revert assets to Presbytery if a constituent Trust (or church) became non-viable and there was no more logical local inheritor.
Deacon	An office in the church carrying the responsibility to exhibit the compassion of the Lord Jesus Christ in a manifold ministry of mercy towards Members and Non-Members of the congregation and strangers on behalf of the church.
Diaconate	The body of Deacons.
Elder	Men who are called to govern the church according to Scripture.
General Assembly	Meeting of Synods.
Installation	Process whereby an Elder or Deacon is attached to a congregation.
IPC Constitution	The Constitution, revised 2014, originally drawn up in 1978 and containing earlier material drawn up by Francis Schaeffer as the constitution of the International Church Presbyterian Reformée.
IPC Practice	The body of practice adopted and drawn up from time to time in the IPC (e.g. questions to be asked of church officers or Members, or parents of infants being baptised.)
Ordination	The setting apart of a person in a church office to follow a calling in the church, which is generally recognised by the church.

Parity	Equality in governmental power.
Pastoral business	The work that an Elder usually does on an individual one-to-one basis, and which by its nature is confidential.
Presbyterian government	A type of Church government by Presbyters or Elders.
Presbytery	A council comprising all Elders within a certain geographic or other designated area.
Pre-separation Protocol	An agreed procedure tailor-made to fit any given situation, the purpose of which is to achieve fairness and orderliness before any congregation separates from IPC.
Session	A council of Elders who rule the local church.
Quorum	Minimum number of people at a meeting to make it valid for conducting business.
Synod	The council of the church that has an authority greater in degree and wider in extent than the presbyteries under it.
Three Forms of Unity	The Heidelberg Catechism, the Belgic Confession and the Canons of Dordrecht.
Trustee	A person in whom property or other things (such as adherence to a certain theological doctrine) is vested on behalf of a body of other persons.
Westminster	The Confession of Faith and the

Confession of Faith   Larger and Shorter Catechisms have been rightly said to be the finest creedal formulations of the Christian Faith that the Church of Christ has yet produced (John Murray). They were drawn up by order of Parliament in the 17th century, and have since been used by thousands of Churches all over the world as the statements of central faith.

III: Model Church Constitution

While the IPC does not mandate a format of local church constitution, the following is given as a suggested model:

We hereby constitute ourselves to be a part of Christ's universal and apostolic Church, recognising the Holy Scriptures to be the inspired Word of God and the supreme authority in matters of faith and life.

Subordination to IPC

The control of the affairs of the Congregation, both spiritual and temporal, shall (subject to any Acts, Regulations or Directions which may subsequently be enacted by the International Presbyterian Church, hereinafter referred to as the 'IPC') be vested in the Session of the congregation (hereinafter referred to as 'the Session'). Such functions shall include all those devolving in terms of the Book of Church Order of the IPC (this may be inspected in the church office on request). Nothing herein shall affect the status of the Session as a council of the Church.

Church Membership

The procedure for church membership shall be subject to the Session and shall be in accord with the Laws of the IPC.

Session

The Session shall consist of the Teaching Elder(s) of the

charge together with the Ruling Elder(s) ordained and admitted to the Session in accordance with the laws of the IPC as expressed in the Book of Church Order. Other Elders and trainees may be associated with the work of the Session as permitted by the law of the Church.

The Session shall lead and nurture the spiritual welfare of the congregation and encourage participation in Christian worship and promote mission and evangelism.

An Elder shall be appointed by agreement of constituent Elders to be Moderator of the Session. In a vacancy or where the Teaching Elder has, for any reason, been granted leave of absence, the Presbytery shall appoint one of its number to act as a temporary Elder (and may do so where a vacancy is anticipated) with all the powers, and to fulfill all the usual functions of the full-time Elders of the church.

It shall be the function of the Moderator to call meetings of the Session and he shall be bound to do so within ten days if requested in writing by a majority of the Elders. Meetings shall normally be held in public with pastoral or disciplinary matters being taken in private by resolution of the Session. The quorum at meetings shall be a majority of Elders including the Moderator. Procedure at meetings shall be in accordance with the law of the Church, subject to which it shall be competent for the Session to frame Standing Orders to regulate its own business. Failing it doing so, its business shall be regulated in terms of the Book of Church Order of the IPC which shall take precedence in areas of dispute.

The Session shall appoint a Clerk. The person so appointed shall hold office during the pleasure of the Session. It shall be the duty of the Clerk to keep regular minutes of the proceedings of the Session and also of the proceedings at the Annual Meeting of the congregation and to maintain these in a permanent record in which each minute, when approved, shall be signed by the Moderator and the Clerk. He shall issue extract minutes when so instructed, and ensure the safe custody of all official records.

The Session Clerk (or another Elder) shall organise Communion services (the dates and times of the services being agreed by the Session).

It should be noted that any document signed by the Clerk in that capacity carries the presumptive approval and authority of the Session.

The Session may arrange for any of its functions to be discharged on its behalf by a committee (retaining nevertheless full responsibility for the diligent discharge thereof). When delegating to a committee with powers, the Session shall cause to be minuted the powers so delegated and any conditions or restrictions applicable to the delegation.

It shall be the duty of the Session to oversee the temporal affairs of the church, through a Diaconate council to which it may devolve decision-making authority for such temporal functions. The Session shall, however, maintain a responsibility to create and maintain in the congregation a commitment to provide, by regular giving, sufficient income to meet the cost of the whole financial and other temporal affairs and obligations of the congregation and to take all necessary and appropriate measures to secure that end.

Diaconate Council

The Diaconate council shall be established as defined by the IPC. It is a decision-making body under authority of the Session and as such shall organise the temporal affairs of the church, together with other responsibilities delegated to it by the Session. Deacons (or council members) shall be expected to participate in meetings, in sub-committees of the Diaconate council and to set an example of Christian leadership in the church family.

The Elders of the church shall be *ex officio* members of the Diaconate council. A Deacon or Elder shall chair meetings of the Diaconate council. The Session shall determine the number of Deacons to serve for 3-year renewable terms. The Diaconate council shall make recommendation to the Session for the co-opting of additional members to fill any vacancies that emerge.

Stated meetings of the Diaconate council shall be intimated in advance at the ordinary services on two consecutive Sundays. The council shall meet for ordinary business quarterly, meetings shall be open to all who wish to attend. A secretary shall prepare and distribute an agenda in advance of meetings.

The agenda shall be agreed and adopted at the commencement of meetings. The secretary shall distribute the minute in advance of the next meeting. The minute shall be agreed (or amended if necessary) and signed at the subsequent meeting of the council. Decisions shall normally be reached by consensus. In the unlikely event of a vote being required, decisions shall be carried by a simple majority of council members who are present. A quorum shall be one Elder, plus three council members. The council shall have capacity to meet additionally as required, intimated as above.

The council has the facility to convene additional sub-committees to support and facilitate its functions as required.

The Session and Diaconate council gratefully recognises that there are a large number of church functions that are readily handled by an individual or small group. These areas of delegated task may report to the Session or Diaconate council where support is required.

Reserved Matters

While maintaining oversight, the Session wishes to empower its sub-committees to make appropriate decisions (as outlined in this document). For clarity, several areas are specifically reserved:

(i) the content, frequency and times of services, outreach and mission;

(ii) staff contracts;

(iii) annual accounts and budget approval;

(iv) decisions on matters of discipline, admission to membership and appointment of Elders.

Church Finances

The church Trust (or recognised legal entity) is the financially competent body of the church. All financial expenditure of the church is subject to the approval of the

Trustees who shall include all Elders.

Appeal

If any question shall arise with reference to the interpretation of any article of this Constitution or the legality of any particular exercise of the powers herein contained, it shall be competent to any person or body interested to apply by petition to the Presbytery of the IPC to adjudicate upon the matter and the judgment of the Presbytery upon such matter shall be final, subject only to appeal to the IPC Synod.

Delegation: it shall be in the power of the IPC or any body to which they may delegate powers at any time, or from time to time, to alter, revoke, amend or modify this Deed of Constitution, in whole or in part, or to substitute a new Deed of Constitution for this Deed of Constitution, subject always to such conditions and provisions relative thereto as the IPC or its delegated body shall determine.

Congregational Meetings

The congregation shall meet at least bi-annually. Items of competent business shall be submitted to the Session Clerk no later than 2 weeks prior to the stated date of a given meeting.

The competent body for amending the church constitution is a majority of voting church Members present at a quorate (one third of communing Members over 18) congregational meeting called by intimation for 2 weeks in advance.

IV: Original IPC Baptismal Vows

The original form of words from Francis Schaeffer's booklet are as follows:

1. Do you acknowledge that you are saved only through faith in Jesus, that you trust not in anything you have done or will ever do, but only in His finished work — His death upon the Cross — by which He took upon Himself the penalty for your sins?

2. Do you realise that baptism is not a saving ordinance, and though it signifies your children's membership in the covenant community, it is not a matter of magic? Do you understand that your children are themselves responsible to receive Christ as Saviour and Lord as they become accountable to Him?

3. Do you in this sacrament covenant together with God to raise your children in the instruction, obedience, and worship of the Lord, to pray for and with them, to keep them in the fellowship of God's people, to be faithful and loving in your home, to be immediate examples of faith, and therefore to do your utmost to lead them to a saving knowledge of Christ at an early age?

4. Do you acknowledge that your children are a gift of God, who are of course to be cherished and enjoyed, but who belong at last not to you but to God? Do you undertake to assist your children in every possible way as they seek to lead a life of devoted service to his Lord and Saviour? Do you, with God's help, undertake not to hinder your children should they feel called to serve God in a far-away place? Do you, with

God's help, undertake not to complain against God should your children die before you?

Congregation:

Do you, the members of this congregation, agree to pray for these parents as they raise their children in the Christian Faith, and to support them in their efforts by providing their children with further examples of obedience and service to God? Should these parents neglect their God-given task, will you in all humility rebuke and correct them?

The 3rd edition BCO wording follows:

(A) PRACTICE ON ADULT BAPTISM: BAPTISMAL VOWS

1.   The practice to be followed for an adult baptism in the IPC is that the candidate should have been prayerfully examined by an Elder beforehand with regard to his or her understanding of baptism and true ability to affirm the following five questions, which are to be put to the candidate in public at the baptismal service:

Q 1. Do you believe that God exists, that He is not an idea or concept in the mind, and that He exists as a personal God, in fact, the three persons of the Father, Son and the Spirit, who have existed forever?

Q 2. Do you know that you have many times done things you know to be wrong and that if God were to judge you as you deserve, He would have to condemn you?

Q 3. Do you believe that Jesus Christ, who has existed forever as the Second Person of the Trinity, became a man and lived a perfect life and that, when He died on the cross and rose again in history, He did everything that was necessary to atone for your sin and restore you to a relationship with God?

Q 4. Have you personally accepted this work of Christ and have you believed the promises of God, such a promise as 'he who believes on the Son has everlasting life', so that you can say without any pride or presumption that you are a child of God and born into His family?

Q 5. Do you now intend to serve Christ and acknowledge His Lordship over your whole life, knowing that you will need to depend on the strength of the Holy Spirit, and knowing that this obedience may be costly to you, but it will not bring any loss to yourself, but rather fulfilment to yourself as a creature made in God's image?

2. Following this, the following question (or a similar one inviting the support of the congregation) may be put to the witnessing congregation, as may be fitting for the occasion:

Q. Will you, [the candidate's] supernatural family, by prayer, witness and love, support [the candidate] as [he or she] undertakes to keep their promises, made before us and before God today?

3. It is usual for a certificate of baptism to be presented by the Session. These are available through the Presbytery, and should be ordered from the Clerk beforehand if the certificate is to be presented at the service.

(B) PRACTICE ON INFANT BAPTISM: BAPTISMAL VOWS

1. The practice to be followed for an infant baptism in the IPC is this. The parents or, where appropriate, a parent or proper legal guardian of the infant to be baptised must be prayerfully examined by an Elder beforehand with regard to his, her or their understanding of baptism and true ability to affirm the following 8 questions, which are to be put to him, her or them in public at a baptismal service:

Q 1. Do you believe that God exists, that He is not an idea or concept in the mind, and that He exists as a personal God, in fact, the three persons of the Father, the Son and the Spirit, who have existed forever?

Q 2. Do you know that you have many times done things you know to be wrong and that if God were to judge you as you deserve, He would have to condemn you?

Q 3. Do you believe that Jesus Christ, who has existed forever as the Second Person of the Trinity, became a man and lived a perfect life and that, when He died on the Cross and rose again in history, He did everything that was necessary to atone for your sin and restore you to a relationship with God?

Q 4. Have you personally accepted this work of Christ and have you believed the
promises of God, such a promise as 'he who believes on the Son has everlasting life', so that you can say without any pride or presumption that you are a child of God born into His family?

Q 5. Do you now intend to serve Christ and acknowledge

His Lordship over your whole life, knowing that you will need to depend on the strength of the Holy Spirit, and knowing that this obedience may be costly to you, but it will not bring any loss to yourself, but rather fulfilment to yourself as a creature made in God's image?

Q 6. Do you undertake to live according to this faith so that you provide a practical example of it?

Q 7. Do you undertake to fulfil your responsibility as parents — a responsibility you have from God — to pray for this child and to teach the truth of God's Word and the way of life commanded by God's Word, so that he may at an early age accept that his salvation comes only from the death of Christ on the cross for his sins? You as parents have this responsibility first and in priority to the Church or any educational establishment.

Q 8. Do you understand that this child is a gift from God, who is of course to be prized and enjoyed, but that the child does not belong to you in any absolute sense but to God, and that therefore your responsibility is to show him that he does belong to God and to establish him in that relationship for his life, so that he may present himself as a living sacrifice to God which is his spiritual service?

This carries with it two important considerations:

(i)   That you will not stand in his way if he feels called to serve God in geographic separation from you?

(ii)   That you will not complain against God if this child dies before you do?

2. Following this, the following question (or a similar one inviting the support of the congregation) may be put to the witnessing congregation:

Q. Will you, [the candidate's] supernatural family, by prayer, witness and love, support [the candidate] as his or her parent(s) undertakes to keep their promises, made before us and before God today?

3. It is usual for a certificate of baptism to be presented by the Session. These are available through the Presbytery, and should be ordered from the Clerk beforehand if the certificate is to be presented at the service.

V: Subsequent Amendments

Amendments to this BCO are considered by the BCO Editorial Committee, a standing committee of Synod and are subject to the approval of Synod.

Amendments, once approved by Synod, will be posted at http://www.ipcsynod.com/bco-amendments

Any amendments to this BCO subsequent to its adoption should be affixed here and will be included in the text of any subsequent edition.

VI: Standing Orders of Standing Committee of Synod

(also BCO Editorial Committee) standing orders*
(Revised 3rd March 2017)

The Synod of 2015 mandated the establishment of a Synod standing committee.
The following standing orders* have been adopted by Synod to direct the work of the committee:

1. The Standing Committee of Synod (SCS) shall function as the BCO Editorial Committee of Synod.

2. The Standing Committee is responsible for investigating, recommending and maintaining formal and/or fraternal relationships with other churches and external organisations.

3. The SCS should include two representatives from each Presbytery or proto-Presbytery one of whom is nominated by the (proto)Presbytery and the other is the (proto)Presbytery moderator or his deputy. The Synod moderator and clerk shall be ex officio members of the committee.

4. The SCS shall, through its clerk be the appropriate place to lodge any and all proposed amendments to the BCO by individual elders or their Presbyteries (note: a seconder is not required for motions from Presbyteries).

5. When a proposed BCO amendment is brought, it should clearly state the following:

a. The reason for the amendment and its intended effect

b. The proposed wording of the amendment and the section(s) of the BCO that are

   proposed for amendment.

c. Who is bringing the proposal.

6. The SCS shall consider all amendments so received and will act on the proposal in one of the following ways:

a. It may bring the proposal to Synod with a recommendation to adopt it

b. It may bring the proposal to Synod with an opinion and/or suggested changes to the amendment with a request to debate the issue(s) at Synod

c. It may bring the proposal with a majority/minority report of the committee, with a request to debate the issue(s) at Synod.

d. It may reject the proposal, giving reasons to whomever submitted it (for instance if it is not compatible with the overriding objective). In this situation the individual could seek their Presbytery's sponsorship for the issue to be brought before Synod.

e. Where the proposed amendment comes from a Presbytery, the outcome will be (a), (b) or (c).

7. The SCS shall consider matters of a denominational nature arising between meetings of Synod, referring other matters to the relevant Presbyteries.

8. Synod expenses shall be authorised by the Standing Committee and shall be the responsibility of its constituent Presbyteries and proto-Presbyteries.

*'Standing orders' do not form part of the BCO but describe accepted practices.

© MMXVII

The International Presbyterian Church

http://www.ipcsynod.com

http://www.ipc.church

Notes

Printed in Great Britain
by Amazon